1

THE NEW TEMPLE SHAKESPEARE

Edited by M. R. Ridley, M.A.

ALL'S WELL
THAT ENDS WELL

by William Shakespeare

London: J. M. DENT & SONS LTD.
New York: E. P. DUTTON & CO. INC.

All rights reserved
Printed in Great Britain
by Morrison & Gibb Ltd., London and Edinburgh
and decorated by

Eric Gill

for

J. M. Dent & Sons Ltd.

Aldine House Bedford St. London
Toronto   .   *Vancouver*
Melbourne   .   *Wellington*
First Published in this edition 1935

Reprinted 1944

Editor's General Note

The Text. The editor has kept before him the aim of presenting to the modern reader the nearest possible approximation to what Shakespeare actually wrote. The text is therefore conservative, and is based on the earliest reliable printed text. But to avoid distraction (*a*) the spelling is modernised, and (*b*) a limited number of universally accepted emendations is admitted without comment. Where a Quarto text exists as well as the First ·Folio the passages which occur only in the Quarto are enclosed in square brackets [ ] and those which occur only in the Folio in brace brackets { }.

Scene Division. The rapid continuity of the Elizabethan curtainless production is lost by the 'traditional' scene divisions. Where there is an essential difference of place these scene divisions are retained. Where on the other hand the change of place is insignificant the scene division is indicated only by a space on the page. For ease of reference, however, the 'traditional' division is retained at the head of the page and in line numbering.

Notes. Passages on which there are notes are indicated by a † in the margin.

Punctuation adheres more closely than has been usual to the 'Elizabethan' punctuation of the early texts. It is often therefore more indicative of the way in which the lines were to be delivered than of their syntactical construction.

Glossaries are arranged on a somewhat novel principle, not alphabetically, but in the order in which the words or phrases occur. The editor is much indebted to Mr J. N. Bryson for his collaboration in the preparation of the glossaries.

Preface

The Text. The play was printed for the first time in the First Folio. It is certainly not a good text, but I am not clear that it merits all the denunciations that have been heaped on it, such as ' our only text and a vile one.' In any event, it is all that we have got and we have to make the best we can of it. There is a considerable number of difficult passages, but whether they are difficult because Shakespeare (or someone else) was writing in a hurry, or because the compositor was incompetent, seems to me often uncertain. The play does not seem to me of sufficient intrinsic importance to demand elaborate consideration of textual problems, and I have therefore adopted freely such recognised emendations as appeared acceptable without always encumbering the notes with acknowledgments ; but I should here acknowledge a general debt to the New Cambridge editors, who are almost the first to make an adequate study of the play, and to try to discover what many obscure passages do in fact mean.

Date of Composition. About this there can be no certainty. Any reader who reads the play with his ears open must be aware of an odd dissonance of impression. Some passages are in the unmistakable late Shakespearean style, the style of *Antony and Cleopatra* applied to a lower order of play; other passages suggest Shakespeare's prentice or even poorer than prentice hand. The conclusion of the New Cambridge editors is that the Folio text is the result of a Jacobean revision in about 1605 of a play which was probably by Shakespeare, but if so contained non-Shakespearean elements, and that the revision was the work of Shakespeare and a collaborator who did most of the work. This is disintegration with a vengeance, since it makes one wonder why Heminge and Condell regarded the play as Shakespeare's at all. Sir Edmund Chambers, on the other hand, does not see ' that any other assumption helps to make this difficult play more intelligible than the assumption of Shakespeare working in an abnormal mood.' He would put the date ' tentatively ' 1602-3. What is, I think, clear is that the play belongs in temper to the period of *Measure for Measure* and *Troilus and Cressida*, and that there is enough textual evidence, in the shape of bad joins, and remarks of which the apropos is absent in the text as we have it, to make one accept some theory of revision.

Source. This at least is clear. It is Boccaccio's tale (3rd day, 9th story, of the *Decamerone*) of *Giglietta di Nerbona*, as englished in Painter's *Palace of Pleasure*.

Duration of Action. Daniel divides the play into eleven days, distributed over three months. I do not think that the details of the division are in fact of much interest to any reader, to whom the ' days ' are clear enough, and who automatically inserts such intervals in the action as are necessary.

Criticism. The critics have not a great deal to say about the play, and many of them give one the impression of reasoning themselves into liking something which by instinct they do not like; and on the whole one is inclined to think that their instinct is juster than their reason. There is about the play more than a tang of the same sour flavour which distinguishes *Troilus and Cressida* and *Measure for Measure*. And both in this play and in *Measure for Measure* a woman whom we are clearly supposed to admire secures her undoubted marital rights by a trick, lending herself to it in one case and devising it in the other. And not all the eulogies that are lavished on Helena, nor the undoubted beauty in which Shakespeare manages to invest her, can disguise the plain fact that with the singleness of aim that characterises all Shakespeare's women she knows exactly what she wants, is determined to get it, and is a hard-headed practical schemer in achieving her aim. This no doubt is inherent in the plot which Shakespeare chose for the basis of his play; but he did choose it, and then gives the impression of trying to throw a pleasanter colour over it, with only modified success.

Johnson.—This play has many delightful scenes, though not sufficiently probable, and some happy characters, though not new, nor produced by any deep knowledge of human nature. Parolles is a boaster and a coward, such as has always been the sport of the stage, but perhaps never raised more laughter or contempt than in the hands of Shakespeare.

I cannot reconcile my heart to Bertram; a man noble without generosity, and young without truth; who marries Helen as a coward, and leaves her as a profligate: when she is dead by his unkindness, sneaks home to a second marriage, is accused by a woman he has wronged, defends himself by falsehood and is dismissed to happiness.

The story of Bertram and Diana had been told before of Mariana and Angelo, and, to confess the truth, scarcely merited to be heard a second time.

Hazlitt.—*All's Well that Ends Well* is one of the most pleasing of our author's comedies. The interest is however more of a serious than a comic nature. The character of Helen is one of great sweetness and delicacy. She is placed in circumstances of the most critical kind, and has to court her husband both as a virgin and a wife : yet the most scrupulous nicety of female modesty is not once violated. There is not one thought or action that ought to bring a blush into her cheeks, or that for a moment lessens her in our esteem.

Swinburne.[1]—The ninth story of the third day of the *Decamerons* is one of the few subjects chosen by Shakespeare—as so many were taken by Fletcher—which are less fit, we may venture to think, for dramatic than for narrative treatment. He has here again shown all possible delicacy of instinct in handling a matter which unluckily it was not possible to handle on the stage with absolute and positive delicacy of feeling or expression. Dr Johnson —in my humble opinion, with some justice; though his verdict has been disputed on the score of undeserved austerity—' could not reconcile his heart to Bertram'; and I, unworthy as I may be to second or support on the score of morality the finding of so great a moralist, cannot reconcile my instincts to Helena. Parolles is even better than Bobadil, as Bobadil is even better than Bessus; and Lafeu is one of the very best old men in all the range of comic art. But the whole charm and beauty of the play, the quality which raises it to the rank of its fellows by making it loveable as well as admirable, we find only in the 'sweet, serene, skylike' sanctity and attraction of adorable old age, made more than ever near and dear to us in the incomparable figure of the old Countess of Roussillon.

[1] From *A Study of Shakespeare*, by permission of W. Heinemann, Ltd

ALL'S WELL THAT ENDS WELL

DRAMATIS PERSONÆ

KING OF FRANCE.
DUKE OF FLORENCE.
BERTRAM, *Count of Rossillion.*
LAFEU, *an old lord.*
PAROLLES, *a follower of Bertram.*
Steward,
LAVACHE, *a clown,* } *servants to the Countess of Rossillion.*
A Page.

COUNTESS OF ROSSILLION, *mother to Bertram.*
HELENA, *a gentlewoman protected by the Countess.*
An old Widow of Florence.
DIANA, *daughter to the Widow.*
VIOLENTA,
MARIANA, } *neighbours and friends to the Widow.*

Lords, Officers, Soldiers, &c., French and Florentine.

SCENE : *Rossillion ; Paris ; Florence ; Marseilles.*

ALL'S WELL THAT ENDS WELL

Act First

Rossillion. The Count's palace

Enter Bertram, the Countess of Rossillion, Helena, and Lafeu, all in black

Cou. In delivering my son from me, I bury a second husband.

Ber. And I in going, madam, weep o'er my father's death anew ; but I must attend his majesty's command, to whom I am now in ward, evermore in subjection. †

Laf. You shall find of the king a husband, madam, you, sir, a father : he that so generally is at all times good, must of necessity hold his virtue to you, whose worthiness would stir it up where it wanted, rather than lack it where there is such abundance. 10

Cou. What hope is there of his majesty's amendment ?

Laf. He hath abandon'd his physicians, madam, under whose practices he hath persecuted time with hope, and finds no other advantage in the process, but only the losing of hope by time.

1

Cou. This young gentlewoman had a father,—O, that
'had'! how sad a passage 'tis!—whose skill was
almost as great as his honesty; had it stretch'd so
far, would have made nature immortal, and death
should have play for lack of work. Would, for the 20
king's sake, he were living! I think it would be
the death of the king's disease.

Laf. How called you the man you speak of, madam?

Cou. He was famous, sir, in his profession, and it was
his great right to be so,—Gerard de Narbon.

Laf. He was excellent indeed, madam: the king very
lately spoke of him admiringly, and mourningly:
he was skilful enough to have liv'd still, if knowledge
could be set up against mortality.

Ber. What is it, my good lord, the king languishes of? 30

Laf. A fistula, my lord.

Ber. I heard not of it before.

Laf. I would it were not notorious. Was this gentlewoman the daughter of Gerard de Narbon?

Cou. His sole child, my lord, and bequeathed to my over-
looking. I have those hopes of her good that her
education promises; her dispositions she inherits,
which makes fair gifts fairer; for where an unclean
mind carries virtuous qualities, there commendations go with pity; they are virtues and traitors 40

too : in her they are the better for their simpleness ;
she derives her honesty, and achieves her goodness.

Laf. Your commendations, madam, get from her tears.

Cou. 'Tis the best brine a maiden can season her praise in.
The remembrance of her father never approaches her
heart but the tyranny of her sorrows takes all livelihood from her cheek.   No more of this, Helena,
go to, no more, lest it be rather thought you affect a
sorrow than to have—

Hel. I do affect a sorrow, indeed, but I have it too.   50

Laf. Moderate lamentation is the right of the dead, ex-
cessive grief the enemy to the living.

Cou. If the living be enemy to the grief, the excess makes
it soon mortal.

Ber. Madam, I desire your holy wishes.

Laf. How understand we that ?   †

Cou. Be thou blest, Bertram, and succeed thy father
In manners, as in shape ! thy blood and virtue
Contend for empire in thee, and thy goodness
Share with thy birthright !   Love all, trust a few,   60
Do wrong to none : be able for thine enemy
Rather in power than use ; and keep thy friend
Under thy own life's key : be check'd for silence,
But never tax'd for speech.   What heaven more will,
That thee may furnish, and my prayers pluck down,

3

Fall on thy head ! Farewell, my lord ;
'Tis an unseason'd courtier ; good my lord,
Advise him.

Laf.　　　　　　He cannot want the best
That shall attend his lord.

Cou. Heaven bless him ! Farewell, Bertram.　　　*Exit*　70

Ber. The best wishes that can be forg'd in your thoughts
be servants to you ! *(to Helena)* Be comfortable to
my mother, your mistress, and make much of her.

Laf. Farewell, pretty lady : you must hold the credit of
your father.　　　　　*Exeunt Bertram and Lafeu*

Hel. O, were that all ! I think not on my father,
And these great tears grace his remembrance more
Than those I shed for him. What was he like ?
I have forgot him : my imagination
Carries no favour in 't but Bertram's.　　　　　80
I am undone, there is no living, none,
If Bertram be away. 'Twere all one
That I should love a bright particular star
And think to wed it, he is so above me :
In his bright radiance and collateral light
Must I be comforted, not in his sphere.
The ambition in my love thus plagues itself :
The hind that would be mated by the lion
Must die for love. 'Twas pretty, though a plague,

4

To see him every hour, to sit and draw   90
His arched brows, his hawking eye, his curls,
In our heart's table ; heart too capable
Of every line and trick of his sweet favour :
But now he 's gone, and my idolatrous fancy
Must sanctify his reliques.   Who comes here ?

Enter Parolles

(*aside*) One that goes with him : I love him for his
    sake,
And yet I know him a notorious liar,
Think him a great way fool, solely a coward ;
Yet these fix'd evils sit so fit in him,
That they take place, when virtue's steely bones   100
Look bleak i' the cold wind : withal, full oft we
    see
Cold wisdom waiting on superfluous folly.   †

Par. Save you, fair queen !

Hel. And you, monarch !   †

Par. No.

Hel. And no.

Par. Are you meditating on virginity ?

Hel. Ay.   You have some stain of soldier in you : let me
    ask you a question.   Man is enemy to virginity ;
    how may we barricado it against him ?   110

Par. Keep him out.

Hel. But he assails, and our virginity, though valiant, in
the defence yet is weak : unfold to us some warlike
resistance.

Par. There is none : man, sitting down before you, will
undermine you and blow you up.

Hel. Bless our poor virginity from underminers and
blowers up ! Is there no military policy, how virgins might blow up men ?

Par. Virginity being blown down, man will quicklier be 120
blown up : marry, in blowing him down again, with
the breach yourselves made, you lose your city. It
is not politic, in the commonwealth of nature, to
preserve virginity. Loss of virginity is rational
increase, and there was never virgin got till virginity
was first lost. That you were made of is metal to
make virgins. Virginity, by being once lost, may
be ten times found ; by being ever kept, it is ever
lost : 'tis too cold a companion ; away with 't !

Hel. I will stand for 't a little, though therefore I die a 130
virgin.

Par. There's little can be said in 't ; 'tis against the rule
of nature. To speak on the part of virginity, is
to accuse your mothers ; which is most infallible
disobedience. He that hangs himself is a virgin :
virginity murders itself, and should be buried in

6

highways out of all sanctified limit, as a desperate
offendress against nature. Virginity breeds mites,
much like a cheese ; consumes itself to the very
paring, and so dies with feeding his own stomach. 140
Besides, virginity is peevish, proud, idle, made of
self-love, which is the most inhibited sin in the
canon. Keep it not, you cannot choose but lose
by 't. Out with 't ! within ten year it will make
itself ten, which is a goodly increase ; and the
principal itself not much the worse : away with 't !

Hel. How might one do, sir, to lose it to her own liking ?

Par. Let me see : marry, ill, to like him that ne'er it
likes. 'Tis a commodity will lose the gloss with
lying ; the longer kept, the less worth : off with 't 150
while 'tis vendible ; answer the time of request.
Virginity, like an old courtier, wears her cap out
of fashion ; richly suited, but unsuitable : just
like the brooch and the tooth-pick, which wear
not now. Your date is better in your pie and
your porridge than in your cheek : and your
virginity, your old virginity, is like one of our
French wither'd pears, it looks ill, it eats drily,
marry, 'tis a wither'd pear ; it was formerly better,
marry, yet 'tis a wither'd pear : will you any thing 160
with it ?

Hel. Not my virginity yet. . . .
    There shall your master have a thousand loves,
    A mother, and a mistress, and a friend,
    A phœnix, captain, and an enemy,
    A guide, a goddess, and a sovereign,
    A counsellor, a traitress, and a dear;
    His humble ambition, proud humility,
    His jarring, concord, and his discord, dulcet;
    His faith, his sweet disaster; with a world   170
    Of pretty, fond, adoptious christendoms,
    That blinking Cupid gossips.   Now shall he—
    I know not what he shall.   God send him well!
    The court's a learning place, and he is one—
Par. What one, i' faith?
Hel. That I wish well.   'Tis pity—
Par. What's pity?
Hel. That wishing well had not a body in't,
    Which might be felt; that we, the poorer born,
    Whose baser stars do shut us up in wishes,   180
    Might with effects of them follow our friends,
    And show what we alone must think, which
        never
    Returns us thanks.

Enter Page

Pa. Monsieur Parolles, my lord calls for you.   *Exit*

Par. Little Helen, farewell : if I can remember thee, I
will think of thee at court.

Hel. Monsieur Parolles, you were born under a charitable
star.

Par. Under Mars, I.

Hel. I especially think, under Mars.   190

Par. Why under Mars ?

Hel. The wars have so kept you under, that you must
needs be born under Mars.

Par. When he was predominant.

Hel. When he was retrograde, I think, rather.

Par. Why think you so ?

Hel. You go so much backward when you fight.

Par. That's for advantage.

Hel. So is running away, when fear proposes the safety :
but the composition that your valour and fear makes 200
in you is a virtue of a good wing, and I like the
wear well.

Par. I am so full of businesses, I cannot answer thee
acutely. I will return perfect courtier ; in the
which, my instruction shall serve to naturalize
thee, so thou wilt be capable of a courtier's counsel,
and understand what advice shall thrust upon thee ;
else thou diest in thine unthankfulness, and thine
ignorance makes thee away : farewell. When thou

hast leisure, say thy prayers ; when thou hast none, †
remember thy friends : get thee a good husband, 211
and use him as he uses thee : so, farewell.   *Exit*

Hel. Our remedies oft in ourselves do lie,
Which we ascribe to heaven : the fated sky
Gives us free scope ; only doth backward pull
Our slow designs, when we ourselves are dull.
What power is it which mounts my love so high ;
That makes me see, and cannot feed mine eye ?
The mightiest space in fortune nature brings
To join like likes, and kiss like native things.   220
Impossible be strange attempts to those
That weigh their pains in sense, and do suppose
What hath been cannot be : who ever strove
To show her merit, that did miss her love ?
The king's disease—my project may deceive me,
But my intents are fix'd, and will not leave me.   *Exit*

SCENE II

Paris.   The King's palace

*Flourish of cornets.   Enter the King of France with
letters, and divers Attendants*

King. The Florentines and Senoys are by the ears ;
Have fought with equal fortune, and continue

      A braving war.

1.L. So 'tis reported, sir.

King. Nay, 'tis most credible ; we here receive it
    A certainty, vouch'd from our cousin Austria,
    With caution, that the Florentine will move us
    For speedy aid ; wherein our dearest friend
    Prejudicates the business, and would seem
    To have us make denial.

1.L.   His love and wisdom,   10
    Approv'd so to your majesty, may plead
    For amplest credence.

King.   He hath arm'd our answer,
    And Florence is denied before he comes :
    Yet, for our gentlemen that mean to see
    The Tuscan service, freely have they leave
    To stand on either part.

2.L.   It well may serve
    A nursery to our gentry, who are sick
    For breathing and exploit.

King.   What's he comes here ?

       Enter Bertram, Lafeu, and Parolles

1.L. It is the Count Rossillion, my good lord,
    Young Bertram.

King.   Youth, thou bear'st thy father's face; **20**
    Frank nature, rather curious than in haste,

  Hath well compos'd thee. Thy father's moral parts
  Mayst thou inherit too ! Welcome to Paris.
Ber. My thanks and duty are your majesty's.
King. I would I had that corporal soundness now,
  As when thy father and myself in friendship
  First tried our soldiership ! He did look far
  Into the service of the time, and was
  Discipled of the bravest : he lasted long,
  But on us both did haggish age steal on,   30
  And wore us out of act. It much repairs me
  To talk of your good father ; in his youth
  He had the wit, which I can well observe
  To-day in our young lords ; but they may jest
  Till their own scorn return to them unnoted
  Ere they can hide their levity in honour :
  So like a courtier, contempt nor bitterness
  Were in his pride, or sharpness ; if they were,
  His equal had awak'd them ; and his honour,
  Clock to itself, knew the true minute when   40
  Exception bid him speak ; and at this time
  His tongue obey'd his hand : who were below him
  He used as creatures of another place,   †
  And bow'd his eminent top to their low ranks,
  Making them proud of his humility,
  In their poor praise he humbled. Such a man

    Might be a copy to these younger times ;
    Which, follow'd well, would demonstrate them now
    But goers backward.

Ber.   His good remembrance, sir,
    Lies richer in your thoughts than on his tomb ;   50
    So in approof lives not his epitaph
    As in your royal speech.

*King.*Would I were with him !   He would always say—
    Methinks I hear him now ; his plausive words
    He scatter'd not in ears, but grafted them,
    To grow there and to bear,—' Let me not live,'—
    This his good melancholy oft began,
    On the catastrophe and heel of pastime,
    When it was out,—' Let me not live,' quoth he,
    ' After my flame lacks oil, to be the snuff   60
    Of younger spirits, whose apprehensive senses
    All but new things disdain ; whose judgements are
    Mere fathers of their garments ; whose constancies
    Expire before their fashions.'   This he wish'd :
    I after him do after him wish too,
    Since I nor wax nor honey can bring home,
    I quickly were dissolved from my hive,
    To give some labourers room.

2.L.   You 're loved, sir ;
    They that least lend it you shall lack you first.

King. I fill a place, I know 't.   How long is 't, count,   70
      Since the physician at your father's died ?
      He was much fam'd.

Ber.   Some six months since, my lord.

King. If he were living, I would try him yet.
      Lend me an arm ; the rest have worn me out
      With several applications : nature and sickness
      Debate it at their leisure.   Welcome, count ;
      My son's no dearer.

Ber.   Thank your majesty.

                     Exeunt.   Flourish

SCENE III

Rossillion.   The Count's palace

Enter Countess, Steward, and Clown

Cou. I will now hear ; what say you of this gentlewoman ?

Ste. Madam, the care I have had to even your content, I
      wish might be found in the calendar of my past
      endeavours ; for then we wound our modesty and
      make foul the clearness of our deservings, when of
      ourselves we publish them.

Cou. What does this knave here ?   Get you gone, sirrah :
      the complaints I have heard of you I do not all

believe : 'tis my slowness that I do not ; for I know
you lack not folly to commit them, and have ability   10
enough to make such knaveries yours.

Clo. 'Tis not unknown to you, madam, I am a poor
fellow.

Cou. Well, sir.

Clo. No, madam, 'tis not so well that I am poor, though
many of the rich are damn'd : but if I may have your
ladyship's good will to go to the world, Isbel the
woman and I will do as we may.

Cou. Wilt thou needs be a beggar ?

Clo. I do beg your good will in this case.   20

Cou. In what case ?

Clo. In Isbel's case and mine own.   Service is no heritage,
and I think I shall never have the blessing of God till
I have issue o' my body ; for they say barnes are
blessings.

Cou. Tell me thy reason why thou wilt marry.

Clo. My poor body, madam, requires it, I am driven on
by the flesh, and he must needs go that the devil
drives.

Cou. Is this all your worship's reason ?   30

Clo. Faith, madam, I have other holy reasons, such as
they are.

Cou. May the world know them ?

15

Clo. I have been, madam, a wicked creature, as you and
all flesh and blood are, and indeed I do marry that I
may repent.

Cou. Thy marriage sooner than thy wickedness.

Clo. I am out o' friends, madam, and I hope to have
friends for my wife's sake.

Cou. Such friends are thine enemies, knave.   40

Clo. You're shallow, madam, in great friends ; for the
knaves come to do that for me which I am aweary of.
He that ears my land spares my team, and gives me
leave to in the crop ; if I be his cuckold, he's my
drudge : he that comforts my wife is the cherisher of
my flesh and blood ; he that cherishes my flesh and
blood loves my flesh and blood ; he that loves my
flesh and blood is my friend : ergo, he that kisses my
wife is my friend.   If men could be contented to be
what they are, there were no fear in marriage, for   50
young Charbon the puritan, and old Poysam the   †
papist, howsome'er their hearts are sever'd in religion,
their heads are both one ; they may joul horns together, like any deer i' the herd.

Cou. Wilt thou ever be a foul-mouth'd and calumnious
knave ?

Clo. A prophet I, madam, and I speak the truth the next
way :

      For I the ballad will repeat,
         Which men full true shall find ;   60
      Your marriage comes by destiny,
         Your cuckoo sings by kind.

Cou. Get you gone, sir : I 'll talk with you more anon.

Ste. May it please you, madam, that he bid Helen come
to you : of her I am to speak.

Cou. Sirrah, tell my gentlewoman I would speak with her,
Helen I mean.

Clo.   Was this fair face the cause, quoth she,
        Why the Grecians sacked Troy ?
     Fond done, done fond,   70
        Was this King Priam's joy ?
     With that she sighed as she stood,
     With that she sighed as she stood,
        And gave this sentence then ;
     Among nine bad if one be good,
     Among nine bad if one be good,
        There 's yet one good in ten.

Cou. What, one good in ten ? you corrupt the song, †
sirrah.

Clo. One good woman in ten, madam, which is a purify-   80
ing o' the song : would God would serve the world
so all the year ! we 'd find no fault with the tithe-

17

woman, if I were the parson : one in ten, quoth a' ?
an we might have a good woman born but one every
blazing star, or at an earthquake, 'twould mend the
lottery well : a man may draw his heart out, ere a'
pluck one.

Cou. You 'll be gone, sir knave, and do as I command you.

Clo. That man should be at woman's command, and yet
no hurt done ! Though honesty be no puritan, yet   90
it will do no hurt ; it will wear the surplice of †
humility over the black gown of a big heart. I
am going, forsooth : the business is for Helen to
come hither.   *Exit*

Cou. Well, now.

Ste. I know, madam, you love your gentlewoman entirely.

Cou. Faith, I do : her father bequeath'd her to me, and
she herself, without other advantage, may lawfully
make title to as much love as she finds : there is
more owing her than is paid, and more shall be paid   100
her than she 'll demand.

Ste. Madam, I was very late more near her than I think
she wish'd me : alone she was, and did communicate
to herself her own words to her own ears ; she
thought, I dare vow for her, they touch'd not any
stranger sense. Her matter was, she loved your
son : Fortune, she said, was no goddess, that had

put such difference betwixt their two estates ; Love
no god, that would not extend his might only where
qualities were level ; . . . queen of virgins, that †
would suffer her poor knight surpris'd without 111
rescue in the first assault or ransom afterward.   This
she deliver'd in the most bitter touch of sorrow
that e'er I heard virgin exclaim in, which I held my
duty speedily to acquaint you withal, sithence, in the
loss that may happen, it concerns you something to
know it.

Cou. You have discharg'd this honestly ; keep it to yourself : many likelihoods inform'd me of this before,
which hung so tottering in the balance, that I could 120
neither believe nor misdoubt.   Pray you, leave me,
stall this in your bosom, and I thank you for your
honest care : I will speak with you further anon.

Exit Steward

Enter Helena

Even so it was with me when I was young :
   If ever we are nature's, these are ours ; this thorn
Doth to our rose of youth rightly belong ;
   Our blood to us, this to our blood is born ;
It is the show and seal of nature's truth,
Where love's strong passion is impress'd in youth :
By our remembrances of days foregone,   130

  Such were our faults, or then we thought them none.
  Her eye is sick on 't, I observe her now.
Hel. What is your pleasure, madam?
Cou.   You know, Helen,
  I am a mother to you.
Hel. Mine honourable mistress.
Cou.   Nay, a mother:
  Why not a mother? When I said 'a mother,'
  Methought you saw a serpent: what's in 'mother,'
  That you start at it? I say, I am your mother,
  And put you in the catalogue of those
  That were enwombed mine: 'tis often seen   140
  Adoption strives with nature, and choice breeds
  A native slip to us from foreign seeds:
  You ne'er oppress'd me with a mother's groan,
  Yet I express to you a mother's care:
  God's mercy, maiden! does it curd thy blood
  To say I am thy mother? What's the matter,
  That this distemper'd messenger of wet,
  The many-colour'd Iris, rounds thine eye?
  Why? that you are my daughter?
Hel.   That I am not.
Cou. I say, I am your mother.
Hel.   Pardon, madam;   150
  The Count Rossillion cannot be my brother:

I am from humble, he from honour'd name ;
No note upon my parents, his all noble :
My master, my dear lord he is, and I
His servant live, and will his vassal die :
He must not be my brother.

Cou.   Nor I your mother ?

Hel. You are my mother, madam ; would you were,—
So that my lord your son were not my brother,—
Indeed my mother ! or were you both our mothers,
I care no more for 't than I do for heaven,   160
So I were not his sister.   Can't no other,
But I your daughter, he must be my brother ?

Cou. Yes, Helen, you might be my daughter-in-law :
God shield you mean it not ! daughter and mother
So strive upon your pulse.   What, pale again ?
My fear hath catch'd your fondness : now I see
The mystery of your loneliness, and find
Your salt tears' head, now to all sense 'tis gross
You love my son ; invention is asham'd,
Against the proclamation of thy passion,   170
To say thou dost not ; therefore tell me true,
But tell me then, 'tis so, for, look, thy cheeks
Confess it th' one to th' other, and thine eyes
See it so grossly shown in thy behaviours,
That in their kind they speak it : only sin

And hellish obstinacy tie thy tongue,
That truth should be suspected.   Speak, is 't so ?
If it be so, you have wound a goodly clew ;
If it be not, forswear 't : howe'er, I charge thee,
As heaven shall work in me for thine avail,   180
To tell me truly.

Hel.   Good madam, pardon me !

Cou. Do you love my son ?

Hel.   Your pardon, noble mistress !

Cou. Love you my son ?

Hel.   Do not you love him, madam ?

Cou. Go not about ; my love hath in 't a bond,
Whereof the world takes note : come, come, disclose
The state of your affection ; for your passions
Have to the full appeach'd.

Hel.   Then, I confess,
Here on my knee, before high heaven and you,
That before you, and next unto high heaven,
I love your son.   190
My friends were poor, but honest ; so 's my love :
Be not offended, for it hurts not him
That he is lov'd of me : I follow him not
By any token of presumptuous suit ;
Nor would I have him, till I do deserve him,
Yet never know how that desert should be :

I know I love in vain, strive against hope ;
Yet, in this captious and intenible sieve,   †
I still pour in the waters of my love,
And lack not to lose still : thus, Indian-like,   200
Religious in mine error, I adore
The sun, that looks upon his worshipper,
But knows of him no more.   My dearest madam,
Let not your hate encounter with my love
For loving where you do : but if yourself,
Whose aged honour cites a virtuous youth,
Did ever, in so true a flame of liking,
Wish chastely, and love dearly, that your Dian   †
Was both herself and love, O then give pity
To her whose state is such, that cannot choose   210
But lend and give where she is sure to lose ;
That seeks not to find that her search implies,
But, riddle-like, lives sweetly where she dies !

Cou. Had you not lately an intent,—speak truly,—
        To go to Paris ?

Hel.   Madam, I had.

Cou.   Wherefore ? tell true.

Hel. I will tell truth ; by grace itself I swear.
        You know my father left me some prescriptions
        Of rare and prov'd effects, such as his reading
        And manifest experience had collected

For general sovereignty ; and that he will'd me   220
In heedfull'st reservation to bestow them,   †
As notes, whose faculties inclusive were,
More than they were in note : amongst the rest,
There is a remedy, approv'd, set down,
To cure the desperate languishings whereof
The king is render'd lost.

Cou.   This was your motive
For Paris, was it ? speak.

Hel. My lord your son made me to think of this ;
Else Paris, and the medicine, and the king,
Had from the conversation of my thoughts   230
Haply been absent then.

Cou.   But think you, Helen,
If you should tender your supposed aid,
He would receive it ? he and his physicians
Are of a mind, he, that they cannot help him,
They, that they cannot help : how shall they credit
A poor unlearned virgin, when the schools,
Embowell'd of their doctrine, have left off
The danger to itself ?

Hel.   There 's something in 't,   †
More than my father's skill, which was the great'st
Of his profession, that his good receipt   240
Shall for my legacy be sanctified

24

By the luckiest stars in heaven, and, would your
    honour
But give me leave to try success, I 'ld venture
The well-lost life of mine on his Grace's cure
By such a day and hour.

Cou.   Dost thou believe 't ?

Hel. Ay, madam, knowingly.

Cou. Why, Helen, thou shalt have my leave and love,
Means and attendants, and my loving greetings
To those of mine in court : I 'll stay at home
And pray God's blessing into thy attempt :   250
Be gone to-morrow ; and be sure of this,
What I can help thee to, thou shalt not miss. *Exeunt*

Act Second

SCENE I

Paris.   The King's palace

*Flourish of cornets. Enter the King, attended with divers
    young Lords taking leave for the Florentine war ; Bertram,
    and Parolles*

*King.*Farewell, young lords, these warlike principles
Do not throw from you, and you, my lords, farewell :

   Share the advice betwixt you; if both gain, all
   The gift doth stretch itself as 'tis receiv'd,
   And is enough for both.

1.L.   'Tis our hope, sir,
   After well-enter'd soldiers, to return
   And find your Grace in health.

King.No, no, it cannot be; and yet my heart
   Will not confess he owes the malady
   That doth my life besiege. Farewell, young lords; 10
   Whether I live or die, be you the sons
   Of worthy Frenchmen: let higher Italy
   (Those bated that inherit but the fall
   Of the last monarchy) see that you come
   Not to woo honour, but to wed it, when
   The bravest questant shrinks; find what you seek,
   That same may cry you loud: I say, farewell.

2.L. Health at your bidding serve your majesty!

King.Those girls of Italy, take heed of them:
   They say, our French lack language to deny 20
   If they demand: beware of being captives
   Before you serve.

Both.   Our hearts receive your warnings.

King.Farewell, come hither to me.   *Exit*

1.L. O my sweet lord, that you will stay behind us!

Par. 'Tis not his fault, the spark,

2.L.   O, 'tis brave wars !

Par. Most admirable, I have seen those wars.

Ber. I am commanded here, and kept a-coil with
    ' Too young,' and ' the next year,' and ' 'tis too early.'

Par. An thy mind stand to 't, boy, steal away bravely.

Ber. I shall stay here the forehorse to a smock,   30
    Creaking my shoes on the plain masonry,
    Till honour be bought up, and no sword worn
    But one to dance with !   By heaven, I 'll steal away.

1.L. There 's honour in the theft.

Par.   Commit it, count.

2.L. I am your accessary, and so, farewell.

Ber. I grow to you, and our parting is a tortur'd body.

1.L. Farewell, captain.

2.L. Sweet Monsieur Parolles !

Par. Noble heroes ; my sword and yours are kin.   Good
    sparks and lustrous, a word, good metals : you shall   40
    find in the regiment of the Spinii one Captain
    Spurio, with his cicatrice, an emblem of war, here
    on his sinister cheek ; it was this very sword
    entrench'd it : say to him, I live ; and observe his
    reports for me.

1.L. We shall, noble captain.   *Exeunt Lords*

Par. Mars dote on you for his novices ! what will ye do ?

Ber. Stay : the king.

27

Re-enter King

Par. Use a more spacious ceremony to the noble lords ;
you have restrain'd yourself within the list of too   50
cold an adieu : be more expressive to them ; for
they wear themselves in the cap of the time, there
do muster true gait ; eat, speak, and move under the
influence of the most receiv'd star, and though the
devil lead the measure, such are to be followed :
after them, and take a more dilated farewell.

Ber. And I will do so.

Par. Worthy fellows, and like to prove most sinewy
sword-men.   *Exeunt Bertram and Parolles*

Enter Lafeu

Laf. (*kneeling*) Pardon, my lord, for me and for my tidings.   60

King. I 'll fee thee to stand up.

Laf. Then here 's a man stands, that has brought his
    pardon.
I would you had kneel'd, my lord, to ask me mercy ;
And that at my bidding you could so stand up.

King. I would I had, so I had broke thy pate,
And ask'd thee mercy for 't.

Laf. Good faith, across : but, my good lord, 'tis thus ;
Will you be cur'd of your infirmity ?

King. No.

Laf. O, will you eat no grapes, my royal fox ?   70

Yes, but you will my noble grapes, an if
My royal fox could reach them : I have seen a medicine
That 's able to breathe life into a stone,
Quicken a rock, and make you dance canary
With spritely fire and motion, whose simple touch
Is powerful to araise King Pepin, nay,   †
To give great Charlemain a pen in 's hand,
And write to her a love-line.

King.   What ' her ' is this ?

Laf. Why, doctor she : my lord, there 's one arriv'd,
If you will see her : now, by my faith and honour,   80
If seriously I may convey my thoughts
In this my light deliverance, I have spoke
With one that, in her sex, her years, profession,
Wisdom and constancy, hath amaz'd me more
Than I dare blame my weakness : will you see her ?
For that is her demand, and know her business ?
That done, laugh well at me.

King.   Now, good Lafeu,
Bring in the admiration, that we with thee
May spend our wonder too, or take off thine
By wondering how thou took'st it.

Laf.   Nay, I'll fit you,   90
And not be all day neither.   *Exit*

King. Thus he his special nothing ever prologues.

Re-enter Lafeu, with Helena

Laf. Nay, come your ways.

King. This haste hath wings indeed.

Laf. Nay, come your ways ;
    This is his majesty, say your mind to him :
    A traitor you do look like, but such traitors
    His majesty seldom fears : I am Cressid's uncle,
    That dare leave two together ; fare you well. *Exit*

King. Now, fair one, does your business follow us ?

Hel. Ay, my good lord. 100
    Gerard de Narbon was my father ;
    In what he did profess, well found.

King. I knew him.

Hel. The rather will I spare my praises towards him ;
    Knowing him is enough. On's bed of death
    Many receipts he gave me, chiefly one,
    Which, as the dearest issue of his practice,
    And of his old experience the only darling,
    He bade me store up, as a triple eye,
    Safer than mine own two : more dear I have so :
    And, hearing your high majesty is touch'd 110
    With that malignant cause, wherein the honour
    Of my dear father's gift stands chief in power,
    I come to tender it, and my appliance,
    With all bound humbleness.

King.   We thank you, maiden,
　　　But may not be so credulous of cure,
　　　When our most learned doctors leave us, and
　　　The congregated college have concluded
　　　That labouring art can never ransom nature
　　　From her inaidible estate ; I say we must not
　　　So stain our judgement, or corrupt our hope,   120
　　　To prostitute our past-cure malady
　　　To empirics, or to dissever so
　　　Our great self and our credit, to esteem
　　　A senseless help, when help past sense we deem.

Hel. My duty then shall pay me for my pains :
　　　I will no more enforce mine office on you ;
　　　Humbly entreating from your royal thoughts
　　　A modest one, to bear me back again.

King. I cannot give thee less, to be call'd grateful :
　　　Thou thought'st to help me, and such thanks I
　　　　　give   130
　　　As one near death to those that wish him live :
　　　But, what at full I know, thou know'st no part ;
　　　I knowing all my peril, thou no art.

Hel. What I can do can do no hurt to try,
　　　Since you set up your rest 'gainst remedy :
　　　He that of greatest works is finisher,
　　　Oft does them by the weakest minister :

31

So holy writ in babes hath judgement shown,
When judges have been babes; great floods have
    flown
From simple sources; and great seas have dried,   140
When miracles have by the greatest been denied.
Oft expectation fails, and most oft there
Where most it promises; and oft it hits
Where hope is coldest, and despair most fits.

King. I must not hear thee: fare thee well, kind maid;
Thy pains not us'd must by thyself be paid:
Proffers not took reap thanks for their reward.

Hel. Inspired merit so by breath is barr'd:
It is not so with Him that all things knows,
As 'tis with us that square our guess by shows;   150
But most it is presumption in us, when
The help of heaven we count the act of men.
Dear sir, to my endeavours give consent,
Of heaven, not me, make an experiment.
I am not an impostor, that proclaim
Myself against the level of mine aim;
But know I think, and think I know most sure,
My art is not past power, nor you past cure.

King. Art thou so confident? within what space
Hop'st thou my cure?

Hel.   The great'st grace lending grace,

Ere twice the horses of the sun shall bring   161
Their fiery torcher his diurnal ring,
Ere twice in murk and occidental damp
Moist Hesperus hath quench'd his sleepy lamp ;
Or four and twenty times the pilot's glass
Hath told the thievish minutes how they pass ;
What is infirm from your sound parts shall fly,
Health shall live free, and sickness freely die.

King. Upon thy certainty and confidence
What darest thou venture ?

Hel.   Tax of impudence,   170
A strumpet's boldness, a divulged shame
Traduc'd by odious ballads : my maiden's name
Sear'd otherwise, ne worse of worst extended   †
With vilest torture let my life be ended.

King. Methinks in thee some blessed spirit doth speak
His powerful sound, within an organ weak :
And what impossibility would slay
In common sense, sense saves another way.
Thy life is dear ; for all, that life can rate
Worth name of life, in thee hath estimate,   180
Youth, beauty, wisdom, courage, all
That happiness and prime can happy call :
Thou this to hazard needs must intimate
Skill infinite, or monstrous desperate.

33

Sweet practiser, thy physic I will try,
That ministers thine own death if I die.

Hel. If I break time, or flinch in property
Of what I spoke, unpitied let me die,
And well deserv'd : not helping, death's my fee ;
But, if I help, what do you promise me ?   190

King. Make thy demand.

Hel.   But will you make it even ?

King. Ay, by my sceptre and my hopes of heaven.

Hel. Then shalt thou give me with thy kingly hand
What husband in thy power I will command :
Exempted be from me the arrogance
To choose from forth the royal blood of France,
My low and humble name to propagate
With any branch or image of thy state ;
But such a one, thy vassal, whom I know
Is free for me to ask, thee to bestow.   200

King. Here is my hand ; the premises observ'd,
Thy will by my performance shall be serv'd :
So make the choice of thy own time ; for I,
Thy resolv'd patient, on thee still rely.
More should I question thee, and more I must,
Though more to know could not be more to trust ;
From whence thou cam'st, how tended on : but rest
Unquestion'd welcome, and undoubted blest.

34

Give me some help here, ho ! If thou proceed
As high as word, my deed shall match thy deed.   210

Flourish.   Exeunt

SCENE II

Rossillion.   The Count's palace

Enter Countess and Clown

Cou. Come on, sir, I shall now put you to the height of
your breeding.

Clo. I will show myself highly fed and lowly taught : I
know my business is but to the court.

Cou. To the court ! why, what place make you special,
when you put off that with such contempt ?   But to
the court !

Clo. Truly, madam, if God have lent a man any manners,
he may easily put it off at court : he that cannot make
a leg, put off 's cap, kiss his hand, and say nothing,   10
has neither leg, hands, lip, nor cap ; and, indeed,
such a fellow, to say precisely, were not for the
court ; but for me, I have an answer will serve all
men.

Cou. Marry, that 's a bountiful answer that fits all
questions.

Clo. It is like a barber's chair, that fits all buttocks, the

35

pin-buttock, the quatch-buttock, the brawn-buttock, or any buttock.

Cou. Will your answer serve fit to all questions ?   20

Clo. As fit as ten groats is for the hand of an attorney, as your French crown for your taffeta punk, as Tib's rush for Tom's forefinger, as a pancake for Shrove Tuesday, a morris for May-day, as the nail to his hole, the cuckold to his horn, as a scolding quean to a wrangling knave, as the nun's lip to the friar's mouth, nay, as the pudding to his skin.

Cou. Have you, I say, an answer of such fitness for all questions ?

Clo. From below your duke to beneath your constable,   30 it will fit any question.

Cou. It must be an answer of most monstrous size that must fit all demands.

Clo. But a trifle neither, in good faith, if the learned should speak truth of it : here it is, and all that belongs to 't. Ask me if I am a courtier : it shall do you no harm to learn.

Cou. To be young again, if we could : I will be a fool in question, hoping to be the wiser by your answer. I pray you, sir, are you a courtier ?   40

Clo. O Lord, sir ! There 's a simple putting off. More, more, a hundred of them.

Cou. Sir, I am a poor friend of yours, that loves you.

Clo. O Lord, sir !   Thick, thick, spare not me.

Cou. I think, sir, you can eat none of this homely meat.

Clo. O Lord, sir !   Nay, put me to 't, I warrant you.

Cou. You were lately whipp'd, sir, as I think.

Clo. O Lord, sir ! spare not me.

Cou. Do you cry, ' O Lord, sir ! ' at your whipping, and
   ' spare not me ' ?   Indeed your ' O Lord, sir ! ' is   50
   very sequent to your whipping : you would answer
   very well to a whipping, if you were but bound to 't.

Clo. I ne'er had worse luck in my life in my ' O Lord,
   sir ! ' I see things may serve long, but not serve ever.

Cou. I play the noble housewife with the time,
   To entertain 't so merrily with a fool.

Clo. O Lord, sir ! why, there 't serves well again.

Cou. An end, sir ; to your business.   Give Helen this
   And urge her to a present answer back :
   Commend me to my kinsmen, and my son :   60
   This is not much.

Clo. Not much commendation to them.

Cou. Not much employment for you, you understand me ?

Clo. Most fruitfully : I am there before my legs.

Cou. Haste you again.   *Exeunt severally*

SCENE III

Paris.   The King's palace

Enter Bertram, Lafeu, and Parolles

Laf. They say miracles are past ; and we have our philo-
sophical persons, to make modern and familiar things
supernatural and causeless.   Hence is it that we
make trifles of terrors, ensconcing ourselves into
seeming knowledge, when we should submit ourselves to an unknown fear.

Par. Why, 'tis the rarest argument of wonder that hath
shot out in our latter times.

Ber. And so 'tis.

Laf. To be relinquish'd of the artists,—   10

Par. So I say both of Galen and Paracelsus.

Laf. Of all the learned and authentic fellows,—

Par. Right so I say.

Laf. That gave him out incurable,—

Par. Why, there 'tis, so say I too.

Laf. Not to be help'd,—

Par. Right, as 'twere a man assur'd of a—

Laf. Uncertain life, and sure death.

Par. Just, you say well ; so would I have said.

Laf. I may truly say, it is a novelty to the world.   20

Par. It is, indeed, if you will have it in showing, you shall
    read it in—what do ye call 't there ?

Laf. A showing of a heavenly effect in an earthly actor.

Par. That 's it, I would have said, the very same.

Laf. Why, your dolphin is not lustier : 'fore me, I speak †
    in respect—

Par. Nay, 'tis strange, 'tis very strange, that is the brief
    and the tedious of it, and he 's of a most facinerious
    spirit that will not acknowledge it to be the—

Laf. Very hand of heaven.   30

Par. Ay, so I say.

Laf. In a most weak—

Par. And debile minister, great power, great transcend-
    ence, which should, indeed, give us a further use to
    be made than alone the recovery of the king, as to
    be—

Laf. Generally thankful.

Par. I would have said it, you say well.   Here comes the
    king.

        Enter King, Helena, and Attendants

Laf. Lustig, as the Dutchman says : I 'll like a maid the   40
    better, whilst I have a tooth in my head : why, he 's
    able to lead her a coranto.

Par. Mort du vinaigre ! is not this Helen ?

Laf. 'Fore God, I think so.

*King.*Go, call before me all the lords in court.
    Sit, my preserver, by thy patient's side,
    And with this healthful hand, whose banish'd sense
    Thou hast repeal'd, a second time receive
    The confirmation of my promis'd gift.
    Which but attends thy naming.   50
                Enter three or four Lords
    Fair maid, send forth thine eye : this youthful parcel
    Of noble bachelors stand at my bestowing,
    O'er whom both sovereign power, and father's voice,
    I have to use : thy frank election make ;
    Thou hast power to choose, and they none to forsake.

Hel. To each of you one fair and virtuous mistress
    Fall, when Love please ! marry to each, but one !

Laf. I 'ld give bay Curtal and his furniture,
    My mouth no more were broken than these boys',
    And writ as little beard.

King.   Peruse them well: 60
    Not one of those but had a noble father.

Hel. Gentlemen,
    Heaven hath through me restor'd the king to health.

All. We understand it, and thank heaven for you.

Hel. I am a simple maid, and therein wealthiest,
    That I protest I simply am a maid.
    Please it your majesty, I have done already :

The blushes in my cheeks thus whisper me,
' We blush that thou shouldst choose ; but, be refus'd,
Let the white death sit on thy cheek for ever ;   70
We 'll ne'er come there again.'

King.   Make choice, and, see.
Who shuns thy love shuns all his love in me.

Hel. Now, Dian, from thy altar do I fly ;
And to imperial Love, that god most high,
Do my sighs stream.   Sir, will you hear my suit ?

1.L. And grant it.

Hel.   Thanks, sir, all the rest is mute.

Laf. I had rather be in this choice than throw ames-ace †
for my life.

Hel. The honour, sir, that flames in your fair eyes,
Before I speak, too threateningly replies :   80
Love make your fortunes twenty times above
Her that so wishes, and her humble love !

2.L. No better, if you please.

Hel.   My wish receive,
Which great Love grant ! and so, I take my leave. †

Laf. Do all they deny her ?   And they were sons of
mine, I 'ld have them whipped, or I would send
them to the Turk to make eunuchs of.

Hel. Be not afraid that I your hand should take ;
I 'll never do you wrong for your own sake :

41

Blessing upon your vows, and in your bed   90
Find fairer fortune, if you ever wed !

Laf. These boys are boys of ice, they 'll none have her :
sure, they are bastards to the English, the French
ne'er got 'em.

Hel. You are too young, too happy, and too good,
To make yourself a son out of my blood.

4.L. Fair one, I think not so.

Laf. There 's one grape yet ; I am sure thy father drunk
wine : but if thou be'st not an ass, I am a youth of
fourteen ; I have known thee already.   100

Hel. (*to Bertram*) I dare not say I take you, but I give
Me and my service, ever whilst I live,
Into your guiding power.   This is the man.

King. Why, then, young Bertram, take her, she 's thy wife.

Ber. My wife, my liege ?   I shall beseech your highness,
In such a business give me leave to use
The help of mine own eyes.

King. Know'st thou not, Bertram, what she has done for
me ?

Ber. Yes, my good lord, but never hope to know
Why I should marry her.   110

King. Thou know'st she has rais'd me from my sickly bed.

Ber. But follows it, my lord, to bring me down
Must answer for your raising ?   I know her well :

42

She had her breeding at my father's charge.
A poor physician's daughter my wife !   Disdain
Rather corrupt me ever !

King. 'Tis only title thou disdain'st in her, the which
I can build up.   Strange is it, that our bloods,
Of colour, weight, and heat, pour'd all together,
Would quite confound distinction, yet stand off   120
In differences so mighty.   If she be
All that is virtuous (save what thou dislik'st)
A poor physician's daughter, thou dislik'st
Of virtue for the name : but do not so :
From lowest place, whence virtuous things proceed,
The place is dignified by the doer's deed :
Where great additions swell's, and virtue none,
It is a dropsied honour.   Good alone
Is good without a name.   Vileness is so :
The property by what it is should go,   130
Not by the title.   She is young, wise, fair ;
In these to nature she's immediate heir ;
And these breed honour : that is honour's scorn,
Which challenges itself as honour's born,
And is not like the sire : honours thrive,
When rather from our acts we them derive
Than our foregoers : the mere word's a slave
Debosh'd on every tomb, on every grave

A lying trophy, and as oft is dumb

Where dust and damn'd oblivion is the tomb   140

Of honour'd bones indeed.   What should be said?

If thou canst like this creature, as a maid,

I can create the rest : virtue and she

Is her own dower ; honour and wealth from me.

Ber. I cannot love her, nor will strive to do't.

*King.*Thou wrong'st thyself, if thou shouldst strive to
       choose.

Hel. That you are well restor'd, my lord, I'm glad :

     Let the rest go.

*King.*My honour's at the stake, which to defeat,

I must produce my power.   Here, take her hand,   150

Proud scornful boy, unworthy this good gift,

That dost in vile misprision shackle up

My love, and her desert ; that canst not dream,

We, poising us in her defective scale,

Shall weigh thee to the beam ; that wilt not know,

It is in us to plant thine honour where

We please to have it grow.   Check thy contempt :

Obey our will, which travails in thy good :

Believe not thy disdain, but presently

Do thine own fortunes that obedient right   160

Which both thy duty owes and our power claims ;

Or I will throw thee from my care for ever

44

Into the staggers, and the careless lapse
Of youth and ignorance ; both my revenge and
    hate
Loosing upon thee, in the name of justice,
Without all terms of pity.   Speak, thine answer.

Ber. Pardon, my gracious lord ; for I submit
My fancy to your eyes : when I consider
What great creation, and what dole of honour,
Flies where you bid it ; I find that she, which late 170
Was in my nobler thoughts most base, is now
The praised of the king, who, so ennobled,
Is as 't were born so.

King.   Take her by the hand
And tell her she is thine : to whom I promise
A counterpoise ; if not to thy estate,
A balance more replete.

Ber.   I take her hand.

King. Good fortune and the favour of the king
Smile upon this contract ; whose ceremony
Shall seem expedient on the now-born brief,
And be perform'd to-night : the solemn feast 180
Shall more attend upon the coming space,
Expecting absent friends.   As thou lov'st her,
Thy love's to me religious ; else, does err.

            Exeunt all but Lafeu and Parolles

45

Laf. Do you hear, monsieur? a word with you.

Par. Your pleasure, sir.

Laf. Your lord and master did well to make his recantation.

Par. Recantation? My lord? my master?

Laf. Ay: is it not a language I speak?

Par. A most harsh one, and not to be understood without
bloody succeeding. My master? 190

Laf. Are you companion to the Count Rossillion?

Par. To any count, to all counts; to what is man.

Laf. To what is count's man: count's master is of another
style.

Par. You are too old, sir; let it satisfy you, you are too
old.

Laf. I must tell thee, sirrah, I write man; to which title
age cannot bring thee.

Par. What I dare too well do, I dare not do.

Laf. I did think thee, for two ordinaries, to be a pretty 200
wise fellow; thou didst make tolerable vent of thy
travel; it might pass: yet the scarfs and the ban-
nerets about thee did manifoldly dissuade me from
believing thee a vessel of too great a burthen. I have
now found thee; when I lose thee again, I care not:
yet art thou good for nothing but taking up, and that
thou 'rt scarce worth.

Par. Hadst thou not the privilege of antiquity upon thee,—

Laf. Do not plunge thyself too far in anger, lest thou
hasten thy trial ; which if—Lord have mercy on thee 210
for a hen !   So, my good window of lattice, fare thee
well : thy casement I need not open, for I look
through thee.   Give me thy hand.

Par. My lord, you give me most egregious indignity.

Laf. Ay, with all my heart, and thou art worthy of it.

Par. I have not, my lord, deserv'd it.

Laf. Yes, good faith, every dram of it, and I will not bate
thee a scruple.

Par. Well, I shall be wiser.

Laf. Ev'n as soon as thou canst, for thou hast to pull at a 220
smack o' the contrary.   If ever thou be'st bound in
thy scarf and beaten, thou shalt find what it is to be
proud of thy bondage.   I have a desire to hold my
acquaintance with thee, or rather my knowledge,
that I may say in the default, he is a man I know.

Par. My lord, you do me most insupportable vexation.

Laf. I would it were hell-pains for thy sake, and my poor
doing eternal : for doing I am past, as I will by thee,
in what motion age will give me leave.   *Exit*

Par. Well, thou hast a son shall take this disgrace off me ; 230
scurvy, old, filthy, scurvy lord !   Well, I must be
patient, there is no fettering of authority.   I 'll beat
him, by my life, if I can meet him with any con-

47

venience, an he were double and double a lord.   I 'll
have no more pity of his age than I would have of—
I 'll beat him, an if I could but meet him again.

Re-enter Lafeu

Laf. Sirrah, your lord and master 's married, there 's news
for you : you have a new mistress.

Par. I most unfeignedly beseech your lordship to make
some reservation of your wrongs : he is my good 240
lord, whom I serve above is my master.

Laf. Who ?   God ?

Par. Ay, sir.

Laf. The devil it is that 's thy master.   Why dost thou
garter up thy arms o' this fashion ? dost make hose
of thy sleeves ? do other servants so ?   Thou wert
best set thy lower part where thy nose stands.   By
mine honour, if I were but two hours younger, I 'ld
beat thee : methinks 't thou art a general offence, and
every man should beat thee : I think thou wast 250
created for men to breathe themselves upon thee.

Par. This is hard and undeserved measure, my lord.

Laf. Go to, sir, you were beaten in Italy for picking a
kernel out of a pomegranate, you are a vagabond, and
no true traveller : you are more saucy with lords and
honourable personages than the commission of your
birth and virtue gives you heraldry.   You are not

worth another word, else I'ld call you knave.   I
leave you.   *Exit*

Par. Good, very good, it is so then : good, very good ;   260
let it be conceal'd awhile.

Re-enter Bertram

Ber. Undone, and forfeited to cares for ever !

Par. What's the matter, sweet-heart ?

Ber. Although before the solemn priest I have sworn,
I will not bed her.

Par. What ? what, sweet-heart ?

Ber. O my Parolles, they have married me !
I'll to the Tuscan wars, and never bed her.

Par. France is a dog-hole, and it no more merits
The tread of a man's foot : to the wars !   270

Ber. There's letters from my mother : what the import
is, I know not yet.

Par. Ay, that would be known.   To the wars, my boy, to
the wars !
He wears his honour in a box unseen,
That hugs his kicky-wicky here at home,
Spending his manly marrow in her arms,
Which should sustain the bound and high curvet
Of Mars's fiery steed.   To other regions
France is a stable, we that dwell in 't jades,
Therefore to the war !   280

49

Ber. It shall be so, I 'll send her to my house,
  Acquaint my mother with my hate to her,
  And wherefore I am fled ; write to the king
  That which I durst not speak. His present gift
  Shall furnish me to those Italian fields,
  Where noble fellows strike : war is no strife
  To the dark house and the detested wife.

Par. Will this capriccio hold in thee, art sure ?

Ber. Go with me to my chamber, and advise me.
  I 'll send her straight away : to-morrow   290
  I 'll to the wars, she to her single sorrow.

Par. Why, these balls bound, there 's noise in it. 'Tis
   hard :
  A young man married is a man that 's marr'd :
  Therefore away, and leave her bravely ; go :
  The king has done you wrong : but, hush, 'tis so.
            Exeunt

SCENE IV

Paris. The King's palace

Enter Helena and Clown

Hel. My mother greets me kindly : is she well ?

Clo. She is not well, but yet she has her health,
  She 's very merry ; but yet she is not well :

But thanks be given, she 's very well and wants
Nothing i' the world ; but yet she is not well.

Hel. If she be very well, what does she ail,
That she 's not very well ?

Clo. Truly, she 's very well indeed, but for two things.

Hel. What two things ?

Clo. One, that she 's not in heaven, whither God send her   10
quickly ! the other, that she 's in earth, from whence
God send her quickly !

Enter Parolles

Par. Bless you, my fortunate lady !

Hel. I hope, sir, I have your good will to have mine own
good fortune.

Par. You had my prayers to lead them on, and to keep
them on, have them still.   O, my knave, how does
my old lady ?

Clo. So that you had her wrinkles, and I her money, I
would she did as you say.   20

Par. Why, I say nothing.

Clo. Marry, you are the wiser man ; for many a man's
tongue shakes out his master's undoing : to say
nothing, to do nothing, to know nothing, and to
have nothing, is to be a great part of your title ;
which is within a very little of nothing.

Par. Away, thou 'rt a knave.

Clo. You should have said, sir, before a knave thou 'rt a
knave : that 's, before me thou 'rt a knave : this had
been truth, sir.   30

Par. Go to, thou art a witty fool, I have found thee.

Clo. Did you find me in yourself, sir ? or were you taught
to find me ? The search, sir, was profitable, and †
much fool may you find in you, even to the world's
pleasure, and the increase of laughter.

Par. A good knave, i' faith, and well fed.
Madam, my lord will go away to-night,
A very serious business calls on him.
The great prerogative and rite of love,
Which, as your due time claims, he does acknowledge, 40
But puts it off to a compell'd restraint ;
Whose want, and whose delay, is strew'd with sweets
Which they distil now in the curbed time,
To make the coming hour o'erflow with joy,
And pleasure drown the brim.

Hel.   What 's his will else ?

Par. That you will take your instant leave o' the king,
And make this haste as your own good proceeding,
Strengthen'd with what apology you think
May make it probable need.

Hel.   What more commands he ?

Par. That, having this obtain'd, you presently   50

Attend his further pleasure.

Hel. In every thing I wait upon his will.

Par. I shall report it so.   *Exit Parolles*

Hel. I pray you come, sirrah.   *Exeunt*

SCENE V

Paris.   The King's palace

Enter Lafeu and Bertram

Laf. But I hope your lordship thinks not him a soldier.

Ber. Yes, my lord, and of very valiant approof.

Laf. You have it from his own deliverance.

Ber. And by other warranted testimony.

Laf. Then my dial goes not true; I took this lark for a
bunting.

Ber. I do assure you, my lord, he is very great in knowledge, and accordingly valiant.

Laf. I have then sinn'd against his experience and trans-
gress'd against his valour, and my state that way   10
is dangerous, since I cannot yet find in my heart
to repent. Here he comes; I pray you, make us
friends; I will pursue the amity.

Enter Parolles

Par. (*to Bertram*) These things shall be done, sir.

Laf. Pray you, sir, who's his tailor?

Par. Sir ?

Laf. O, I know him well; ay, sir, he, sir, 's a good
workman, a very good tailor.

Ber. *(aside to Parolles)* Is she gone to the king ?

Par. She is.   20

Ber. Will she away to-night ?

Par. As you 'll have her.

Ber. I have writ my letters, casketed my treasure
Given order for our horses, and to-night,
When I should take possession of the bride,
End ere I do begin.

Laf. A good traveller is something at the latter end of a
dinner, but one that lies three thirds, and uses a
known truth to pass a thousand nothings with,
should be once heard, and thrice beaten. God   30
save you, captain.

Ber. Is there any unkindness between my lord and you,
monsieur ?

Par. I know not how I have deserved to run into my lord's
displeasure.

Laf. You have made shift to run into 't, boots and spurs
and all; like him that leap'd into the custard, and
out of it you 'll run again, rather than suffer question
for your residence.

Ber. It may be you have mistaken him, my lord.   40

Laf. And shall do so ever, though I took him at's
prayers. Fare you well, my lord, and believe this
of me, there can be no kernel in this light nut ; the
soul of this man is his clothes. Trust him not in
matter of heavy consequence ; I have kept of them
tame, and know their natures. Farewell, monsieur,
I have spoken better of you than you have or will
to deserve at my hand, but we must do good against
evil.   *Exit*

Par. An idle lord, I swear.   50

Ber. I think so.

Par. Why, do you not know him ?

Ber. Yes, I do know him well, and common speech
Gives him a worthy pass.   Here comes my clog.

Enter Helena

Hel. I have, sir, as I was commanded from you,
Spoke with the king, and have procur'd his leave
For present parting ; only he desires
Some private speech with you.

Ber.   I shall obey his will.
You must not marvel, Helen, at my course,
Which holds not colour with the time, nor does   60
The ministration and required office
On my particular.   Prepar'd I was not
For such a business, therefore am I found

So much unsettled : this drives me to entreat you,
That presently you take your way for home,
And rather muse than ask why I entreat you,
For my respects are better than they seem,
And my appointments have in them a need
Greater than shows itself at the first view
To you that know them not.   This to my mother :   70

Giving a letter

'Twill be two days ere I shall see you ; so,
I leave you to your wisdom.

Hel.   Sir, I can nothing say,
But that I am your most obedient servant.

Ber. Come, come, no more of that.

Hel.   And ever shall
With true observance seek to eke out that
Wherein toward me my homely stars have fail'd
To equal my great fortune.

Ber.   Let that go :
My haste is very great : farewell ; hie home.

Hel. Pray, sir, your pardon.

Ber.   Well, what would you say ?

Hel. I am not worthy of the wealth I owe,   80
Nor dare I say 'tis mine ; and yet it is ;
But, like a timorous thief, most fain would steal
What law does vouch mine own.

Ber.   What would you have ?

Hel. Something, and scarce so much : nothing, indeed.
I would not tell you what I would, my lord : faith,
yes ;
Strangers and foes do sunder, and not kiss.

Ber. I pray you, stay not, but in haste to horse.

Hel. I shall not break your bidding, good my lord.

Ber. Where are my other men ?   Monsieur, farewell !

                                    Exit Helena

Go thou toward home, where I will never come,   90
Whilst I can shake my sword, or hear the drum.
Away, and for our flight.

Par.   Bravely, coragio !   *Exeunt*

Act Third

SCENE I

Florence.   The Duke's palace

*Flourish.   Enter the Duke of Florence, attended ; the two
Frenchmen, with a troop of soldiers*

Du. So that from point to point now have you heard
The fundamental reasons of this war,

Whose great decision hath much blood let forth
And more thirsts after.

1.L.   Holy seems the quarrel
Upon your Grace's part ; black and fearful
On the opposer.

Du. Therefore we marvel much our cousin France
Would in so just a business shut his bosom
Against our borrowing prayers.

2.L.   Good my lord,
The reasons of our state I cannot yield,   10
But like a common and an outward man,
That the great figure of a council frames
By self-unable motion, therefore dare not
Say what I think of it, since I have found
Myself in my incertain grounds to fail
As often as I guess'd.

Du.   Be it his pleasure.

1.L. But I am sure the younger of our nature,
That surfeit on their ease, will day by day
Come here for physic.

Du.   Welcome shall they be ;
And all the honours that can fly from us   20
Shall on them settle.   You know your places well ;
When better fall, for your avails they fell :
To-morrow to the field.   *Flourish. Exeunt*

58

SCENE II

Rossillion.   The Count's palace

Enter Countess and Clown

Cou. It hath happen'd all as I would have had it, save that
he comes not along with her.

Clo. By my troth, I take my young lord to be a very
melancholy man.

Cou. By what observance, I pray you?

Clo. Why, he will look upon his boot and sing ; mend
the ruff and sing, ask questions and sing, pick his
teeth and sing.   I know a man that had this trick
of melancholy sold a goodly manor for a song.

Cou. Let me see what he writes, and when he means to   10
come.   *Opening a letter*

Clo. I have no mind to Isbel since I was at court.   Our
old lings, and our Isbels o' the country, are nothing †
like your old ling and your Isbels o' the court : the
brains of my Cupid's knock'd out, and I begin to
love, as an old man loves money, with no stomach.

Cou. What have we here?

Clo. E'en that you have there.   *Exit*

Cou. (*reads*) I have sent you a daughter-in-law : she hath
recovered the king, and undone me.   I have wedded   20

59

her, not bedded her, and sworn to make the 'not'
eternal. You shall hear I am run away, know it
before the report come. If there be breadth enough
in the world, I will hold a long distance. My duty
to you.

Your unfortunate son,
BERTRAM.

This is not well, rash and unbridled boy,
To fly the favours of so good a king,
To pluck his indignation on thy head   30
By the misprising of a maid too virtuous
For the contempt of empire.

Re-enter Clown

Clo. O madam, yonder is heavy news within between
two soldiers and my young lady!

Cou. What is the matter?

Clo. Nay, there is some comfort in the news, some comfort, your son will not be kill'd so soon as I thought
he would.

Cou. Why should he be kill'd?

Clo. So say I, madam, if he run away, as I hear he does: 40
the danger is in standing to 't; that's the loss of
men, though it be the getting of children. Here
they come will tell you more: for my part, I only
hear your son was run away.   *Exit*

60

Enter Helena and two Gentlemen

1.*G.* Save you, good madam.

Hel. Madam, my lord is gone, for ever gone.

2.*G.* Do not say so.

Cou. Think upon patience.   Pray you, gentlemen,
     I have felt so many quirks of joy and grief,
     That the first face of neither, on the start,   50
     Can woman me unto 't : where is my son, I pray you ?

2.*G.* Madam, he 's gone to serve the duke of Florence,
     We met him thitherward, from thence we came ;
     And, after some dispatch in hand at court,
     Thither we bend again.

Hel. Look on his letter, madam, here 's my passport.
     (*reads*) When thou canst get the ring upon my
     finger, which never shall come off, and show me a
     child begotten of thy body, that I am father to,
     then call me husband : but in such a ' then ' I write   60
     a ' never.'
     This is a dreadful sentence.

Cou. Brought you this letter, gentlemen ?

1.*G.*   Ay, madam ;
     And for the contents' sake are sorry for our pains.

Cou. I prithee, lady, have a better cheer ;
     If thou engrossest all the griefs are thine,
     Thou robb'st me of a moiety : he was my son ;

But I do wash his name out of my blood,
And thou art all my child.   Towards Florence is he?

2.G. Ay, madam.

Cou.   And to be a soldier?   70

2.G. Such is his noble purpose, and, believe 't,
The Duke will lay upon him all the honour
That good convenience claims.

Cou.   Return you thither?

1.G. Ay, madam, with the swiftest wing of speed.

Hel. (*reads*) Till I have no wife, I have nothing in France.
'Tis bitter.

Cou. Find you that there?

Hel.   Ay, madam.

1.G. 'Tis but the boldness of his hand, haply, which his
heart was not consenting to.

Cou. Nothing in France, until he have no wife!   80
There 's nothing here that is too good for him
But only she, and she deserves a lord
That twenty such rude boys might tend upon
And call her hourly mistress.   Who was with him?

1.G. A servant only, and a gentleman
Which I have sometime known.

Cou.   Parolles, was it not?

1.G. Ay, my good lady, he.

Cou. A very tainted fellow, and full of wickedness.

My son corrupts a well-derived nature
With his inducement.

1.G.   Indeed, good lady,
The fellow has a deal of that too much,   90
Which holds him much to have.

Cou. Y' are welcome, gentlemen.
I will entreat you, when you see my son,
To tell him that his sword can never win
The honour that he loses : more I 'll entreat you
Written to bear along.

2.G.   We serve you, madam,
In that and all your worthiest affairs.

Cou. Not so, but as we change our courtesies.
Will you draw near ?   *Exeunt Countess and Gentlemen*

Hel. ' Till I have no wife, I have nothing in France.'   100
Nothing in France, until he has no wife !
Thou shalt have none, Rossillion, none in France ;
Then hast thou all again.   Poor lord ! is 't I
That chase thee from thy country, and expose
Those tender limbs of thine to the event
Of the none-sparing war ? and is it I
That drive thee from the sportive court, where thou
Wast shot at with fair eyes, to be the mark
Of smoky muskets ?   O you leaden messengers,
That ride upon the violent speed of fire,   110

Fly with false aim, move the still-peering air,
That sings with piercing, do not touch my lord.
Whoever shoots at him, I set him there ;
Whoever charges on his forward breast,
I am the caitiff that do hold him to 't ;
And, though I kill him not, I am the cause
His death was so effected : better 'twere
I met the ravin lion when he roar'd
With sharp constraint of hunger ; better 'twere
That all the miseries which nature owes   120
Were mine at once. No, come thou home, Rossillion,
Whence honour but of danger wins a scar,
As oft it loses all : I will be gone ;
My being here it is that holds thee hence :
Shall I stay here to do 't ? no, no, although
The air of paradise did fan the house,
And angels offic'd all : I will be gone,
That pitiful rumour may report my flight,
To consolate thine ear.   Come night, end day ;
For with the dark (poor thief) I 'll steal away. *Exit* 130

SCENE III

Florence.   Before the Duke's palace

*Flourish.   Enter the Duke of Florence, Bertram, Parolles,
Soldiers, Drum, and Trumpets*

Du. The general of our horse thou art, and we,
Great in our hope, lay our best love and credence
Upon thy promising fortune.

Ber.   Sir, it is
A charge too heavy for my strength, but yet
We'll strive to bear it for your worthy sake,
To the extreme edge of hazard.

Du.   Then go thou forth,
And fortune play upon thy prosperous helm,
As thy auspicious mistress !

Ber.   This very day,
Great Mars, I put myself into thy file :
Make me but like my thoughts, and I shall prove   10
A lover of thy drum, hater of love.   *Exeunt*

SCENE IV

Rossillion.   The Count's palace

Enter Countess and Steward

Cou. Alas ! and would you take the letter of her ?
      Might you not know she would do as she has done,
      By sending me a letter ?   Read it again.
Ste. (*reads*) I am Saint Jaques' pilgrim, thither gone :
      Ambitious love hath so in me offended,
      That barefoot plod I the cold ground upon,
      With sainted vow my faults to have amended.
      Write, write, that from the bloody course of war
      My dearest master, your dear son, may hie :
      Bless him at home in peace, whilst I from far   10
      His name with zealous fervour sanctify :
      His taken labours bid him me forgive ;
      I, his despiteful Juno, sent him forth
      From courtly friends with camping foes to live,
      Where death and danger dogs the heels of worth :
      He is too good and fair for death, and me,
      Whom I myself embrace to set him free.
Cou. Ah, what sharp stings are in her mildest words !
      Rinaldo, you did never lack advice so much,
      As letting her pass so : had I spoke with her,   20

66

I could have well diverted her intents,
Which thus she hath prevented.

Ste.   Pardon me, madam :
If I had given you this at over-night,
She might have been o'erta'en ; and yet she writes,
Pursuit would be but vain.

Cou.   What angel shall
Bless this unworthy husband ? he cannot thrive,
Unless her prayers, whom heaven delights to hear
And loves to grant, reprieve him from the wrath
Of greatest justice.   Write, write, Rinaldo,
To this unworthy husband of his wife ;   30
Let every word weigh heavy of her worth
That he does weigh too light : my greatest grief,
Though little he do feel it, set down sharply.
Dispatch the most convenient messenger :
When haply he shall hear that she is gone,
He will return, and hope I may that she,
Hearing so much, will speed her foot again,
Led hither by pure love : which of them both
Is dearest to me, I have no skill in sense
To make distinction : provide this messenger :   40
My heart is heavy, and mine age is weak ;
Grief would have tears, and sorrow bids me speak.

                                        Exeunt

Florence. Without the walls. A tucket afar off

Enter an old Widow of Florence, Diana, Violenta, and Mariana, with other Citizens

Wid. Nay, come, for if they do approach the city, we shall lose all the sight.

Dia. They say the French count has done most honourable service.

Wid. It is reported that he has taken their greatest commander, and that with his own hand he slew the Duke's brother. (*Tucket.*) We have lost our labour; they are gone a contrary way: hark! you may know by their trumpets.

Mar. Come, let's return again, and suffice ourselves with the report of it. Well, Diana, take heed of this French earl: the honour of a maid is her name; and no legacy is so rich as honesty.

Wid. I have told my neighbour how you have been solicited by a gentleman his companion.

Mar. I know that knave, hang him, one Parolles, a filthy officer he is in those suggestions for the young earl. Beware of them, Diana; their promises, enticements, oaths, tokens, and all these engines of lust,

68

are not the things they go under : many a maid hath   20
been seduced by them, and the misery is example,
that so terrible shows in the wreck of maidenhood,
cannot for all that dissuade succession, but that
they are limed with the twigs that threaten them.
I hope I need not to advise you further, but I hope
your own grace will keep you where you are, though
there were no further danger known, but the modesty
which is so lost.

Dia. You shall not need to fear me.

Wid. I hope so.   30

Enter Helena, *disguised like a Pilgrim*

Look, here comes a pilgrim : I know she will lie at
my house, thither they send one another : I 'll
question her.   God save you, pilgrim, whither are
you bound ?

Hel. To Saint Jaques le Grand.
Where do the palmers lodge, I do beseech you ?

Wid. At the Saint Francis here beside the port.

Hel. Is this the way ?

Wid. Ay, marry, is 't.   (*A march afar.*)   Hark you ! they
      come this way.
If you will tarry, holy pilgrim,   40
But till the troops come by,
I will conduct you where you shall be lodg'd ;

       The rather, for I think I know your hostess
       As ample as myself.

Hel.   Is it yourself ?

Wid. If you shall please so, pilgrim.

Hel. I thank you, and will stay upon your leisure.

Wid. You came, I think, from France ?

Hel.   I did so.

Wid. Here you shall see a countryman of yours
       That has done worthy service.

Hel.   His name, I pray you ?

Dia. The Count Rossillion : know you such a one ?   50

Hel. But by the ear, that hears most nobly of him :
       His face I know not.

Dia.   Whatsome'er he is,
       He 's bravely taken here.   He stole from France,
       As 'tis reported, for the king had married him
       Against his liking.   Think you it is so ?

Hel. Ay, surely, mere the truth : I know his lady.

Dia. There is a gentleman that serves the count
       Reports but coarsely of her.

Hel.   What 's his name ?

Dia. Monsieur Parolles.

Hel.   O, I believe with him,
       In argument of praise, or to the worth   60
       Of the great count himself, she is too mean

    To have her name repeated : all her deserving
    Is a reserved honesty, and that
    I have not heard examin'd.

Dia.   Alas, poor lady,
    'Tis a hard bondage to become the wife
    Of a detesting lord.

Wid. I warrant good creature, wheresoe'er she is,
    Her heart weighs sadly : this young maid might do her
    A shrewd turn, if she pleas'd.

Hel.   How do you mean ?
    May be the amorous count solicits her   70
    In the unlawful purpose.

Wid.   He does indeed,
    And brokes with all that can in such a suit
    Corrupt the tender honour of a maid :
    But she is arm'd for him, and keeps her guard
    In honestest defence.

Mar.   The gods forbid else !

Wid. So, now they come :

                Drum and Colours
      Enter Bertram, Parolles, and the whole army
    That is Antonio, the Duke's eldest son ;
    That, Escalus.

Hel.   Which is the Frenchman ?

Dia.   He,

That with the plume, 'tis a most gallant fellow.
I would he lov'd his wife : if he were honester   80
He were much goodlier : is 't not a handsome gentle-
  man ?

Hel. I like him well.

Dia. 'Tis pity he is not honest : yond 's that same knave
That leads him to these places : were I his lady,
I would poison that vile rascal.

Hel.   Which is he ?

Dia. That jack-an-apes with scarfs : why is he melancholy ?

Hel. Perchance he 's hurt i' the battle.

Par. Lose our drum ? well !

Mar. He 's shrewdly vex'd at something : look, he has
  spied us.

Wid. Marry, hang you !   90

Mar. And your courtesy, for a ring-carrier !

        Exeunt Bertram, Parolles, and army

Wid. The troop is past.   Come, pilgrim, I will bring you
Where you shall host : of enjoin'd penitents
There 's four or five, to great Saint Jaques bound,
Already at my house.

Hel.   I humbly thank you :
Please it this matron, and this gentle maid,
To eat with us to-night, the charge and thanking
Shall be for me, and, to requite you further,

I will bestow some precepts of this virgin
Worthy the note.

Both.   We 'll take your offer kindly.   100

Exeunt

SCENE VI

Camp before Florence

Enter Bertram and the two French Lords

2.*L.* Nay, good my lord, put him to 't ; let him have his
way.

1.*L.* If your lordship find him not a hilding, hold me no
more in your respect.

2.*L.* On my life, my lord, a bubble.

Ber. Do you think I am so far deceived in him ?

2.*L.* Believe it, my lord, in mine own direct knowledge,
without any malice, but to speak of him as my
kinsman, he 's a most notable coward, an infinite
and endless liar, an hourly promise-breaker, the   10
owner of no one good quality worthy your lordship's entertainment.

1.*L.* It were fit you knew him, lest, reposing too far in
his virtue, which he hath not, he might at some great
and trusty business, in a main danger, fail you.

73

Ber. I would I knew in what particular action to try him.

1.*L.* None better than to let him fetch off his drum, which you hear him so confidently undertake to do.

2.*L.* I, with a troop of Florentines, will suddenly surprise him ; such I will have whom I am sure he knows not 20 from the enemy : we will bind and hoodwink him so, that he shall suppose no other but that he is carried into the leaguer of the adversaries, when we bring him to our own tents : be but your lordship present at his examination, if he do not, for the promise of his life, and in the highest compulsion of base fear, offer to betray you, and deliver all the intelligence in his power against you, and that with the divine forfeit of his soul upon oath, never trust my judgement in any thing. 30

1.*L.* O, for the love of laughter, let him fetch his drum, he says he has a stratagem for 't : when your lordship sees the bottom of his success in 't, and to what metal this counterfeit lump of ore will be melted, if you give him not John Drum's entertainment, your inclining cannot be removed. Here he comes.

Enter Parolles

2.*L.* (*aside to Ber.*) O, for the love of laughter, hinder not the honour of his design, let him fetch off his drum in any hand.

Ber. How now, monsieur? this drum sticks sorely in   40
    your disposition.

1.L. A pox on 't, let it go, 'tis but a drum.

Par. 'But a drum'! is 't 'but a drum'? A drum so
    lost!   There was excellent command,—to charge in
    with our horse upon our own wings, and to rend
    our own soldiers!

1.L. That was not to be blam'd in the command of the
    service: it was a disaster of war that Cæsar him-
    self could not have prevented, if he had been there
    to command.   50

Ber. Well, we cannot greatly condemn our success: some
    dishonour we had in the loss of that drum, but it is
    not to be recovered.

Par. It might have been recovered.

Ber. It might, but it is not now.

Par. It is to be recovered, but that the merit of service is
    seldom attributed to the true and exact performer,
    I would have that drum or another, or ' hic jacet.'

Ber. Why, if you have a stomach, to 't, monsieur: if you
    think your mystery in stratagem can bring this instru-   60
    ment of honour again into his native quarter, be
    magnanimous in the enterprise and go on; I will
    grace the attempt for a worthy exploit: if you speed
    well in it, the Duke shall both speak of it, and extend

to you what further becomes his greatness, even to
the utmost syllable of your worthiness.

Par. By the hand of a soldier, I will undertake it.

Ber. But you must not now slumber in it.

Par. I 'll about it this evening, and I will presently pen
down my dilemmas, encourage myself in my cer-   70
tainty, put myself into my mortal preparation ; and
by midnight look to hear further from me.

Ber. May I be bold to acquaint his Grace you are gone
about it ?

Par. I know not what the success will be, my lord, but
the attempt I vow.

Ber. I know thou 'rt valiant ; and, to the possibility of
thy soldiership, will subscribe for thee.   Farewell.

Par. I love not many words.   *Exit*

2.L. No more than a fish loves water. Is not this a   80
strange fellow, my lord, that so confidently seems
to undertake this business, which he knows is not
to be done, damns himself to do, and dares better
be damn'd than to do 't ?

1.L. You do not know him, my lord, as we do : certain
it is, that he will steal himself into a man's favour,
and for a week escape a great deal of discoveries, but
when you find him out, you have him ever after.

Ber. Why, do you think he will make no deed at all

    of this that so seriously he does address himself   90
    unto ?

.L. None in the world, but return with an invention,
    and clap upon you two or three probable lies : but
    we have almost emboss'd him ; you shall see his fall
    to-night ; for indeed he is not for your lordship's
    respect.

.L. We 'll make you some sport with the fox ere we
    case him. He was first smok'd by the old lord
    Lafeu ; when his disguise and he is parted, tell me
    what a sprat you shall find him, which you shall see 100
    this very night.

.L. I must go look my twigs : he shall be caught.

Ber. Your brother he shall go along with me.

.L. As 't please your lordship : I 'll leave you.   *Exit*

Ber. Now will I lead you to the house, and show you
    The lass I spoke of.

.L.   But you say she 's honest.

Ber. That 's all the fault : I spoke with her but once
    And found her wondrous cold, but I sent to her,
    By this same coxcomb that we have i' the wind
    Tokens and letters, which she did re-send,   110
    And this is all I have done. She 's a fair creature :
    Will you go see her ?

.L.   With all my heart, my lord. *Exeunt*

SCENE VII

Florence.   The Widow's house

Enter Helena and Widow

Hel. If you misdoubt me that I am not she,
    I know not how I shall assure you further,
    But I shall lose the grounds I work upon.

Wid. Though my estate be fallen, I was well born,
    Nothing acquainted with these businesses ;
    And would not put my reputation now
    In any staining act.

Hel.   Nor would I wish you.
    First give me trust, the count he is my husband,
    And what to your sworn counsel I have spoken
    Is so from word to word ; and then you cannot,   I
    By the good aid that I of you shall borrow,
    Err in bestowing it.

Wid.   I should believe you ;
    For you have show'd me that which well approves
    You 're great in fortune.

Hel.   Take this purse of gold,
    And let me buy your friendly help thus far,
    Which I will over-pay, and pay again,
    When I have found it.   The count he woos your daughter,

Lays down his wanton siege before her beauty,
Resolv'd to carry her : let her in fine consent,
As we 'll direct her how 'tis best to bear it.   20
Now this important blood will nought deny
That she 'll demand : a ring the county wears,
That downward hath succeeded in his house
From son to son, some four or five descents,
Since the first father wore it : this ring he holds
In most rich choice ; yet in his idle fire,
To buy his will, it would not seem too dear,
Howe'er repented after.

Wid.   Now I see
The bottom of your purpose.

Hel. You see it lawful, then : it is no more,   30
But that your daughter, ere she seems as won,
Desires this ring ; appoints him an encounter ;
In fine, delivers me to fill the time,
Herself most chastely absent : after this,
To marry her, I 'll add three thousand crowns
To what is past already.

Wid.   I have yielded :
Instruct my daughter how she shall persever,
That time and place with this deceit so lawful
May prove coherent.   Every night he comes
With musics of all sorts, and songs compos'd   40

79

  To her unworthiness : it nothing steads us
  To chide him from our eaves, for he persists
  As if his life lay on 't.

Hel.   Why then to-night
  Let us assay our plot, which, if it speed,
  Is wicked meaning in a lawful deed,
  And lawful meaning in a lawful act,
  Where both not sin, and yet a sinful fact :
  But let 's about it.   *Exeun*

Act Fourth

SCENE I

Without the Florentine camp

*Enter Second French Lord, with five or six other
Soldiers in ambush*

2.*L.* He can come no other way but by this hedge-corner.
 When you sally upon him, speak what terrible language you will : though you understand it not yourselves, no matter ; for we must not seem to understand him, unless some one among us whom we
 must produce for an interpreter.

1.*S.* Good captain, let me be the interpreter.

2.*L.* Art not acquainted with him ? knows he not thy
    voice ?

1.*S.* No, sir, I warrant you.   10

2.*L.* But what linsey-woolsey hast thou to speak to us
    again ?

1.*S.* E'en such as you speak to me.

2.*L.* He must think us some band of strangers i' the
    adversary's entertainment.   Now he hath a smack
    of all neighbouring languages ; therefore we must
    every one be a man of his own fancy, not to know
    what we speak one to another ; so we seem to know,
    is to know straight our purpose : choughs' language,
    gabble enough, and good enough.   As for you,   20
    interpreter, you must seem very politic.   But couch,
    ho ! here he comes, to beguile two hours in a sleep,
    and then to return and swear the lies he forges.

Enter Parolles

Par. Ten o'clock : within these three hours 'twill be time
    enough to go home.   What shall I say I have done ?
    It must be a very plausive invention that carries it :
    they begin to smoke me ; and disgraces have of late
    knock'd too often at my door.   I find my tongue is
    too foolhardy ; but my heart hath the fear of Mars
    before it and of his creatures, not daring the reports   30
    of my tongue.

2.L. This is the first truth that e'er thine own tongue was guilty of.

Par. What the devil should move me to undertake the recovery of this drum, being not ignorant of the impossibility, and knowing I had no such purpose? I must give myself some hurts, and say I got them in exploit : yet slight ones will not carry it ; they will say, ' Came you off with so little ? ' and great ones I dare not give. Wherefore, what's the instance?   40 Tongue, I must put you into a butter-woman's mouth, and buy myself another of Bajazet's mule, if † you prattle me into these perils.

2.L. Is it possible he should know what he is, and be that he is?

Par. I would the cutting of my garments would serve the turn, or the breaking of my Spanish sword.

2.L. We cannot afford you so.

Par. Or the baring of my beard ; and to say it was in stratagem.   50

2.L. 'Twould not do.

Par. Or to drown my clothes, and say I was stripp'd.

2.L. Hardly serve.

Par. Though I swore I leap'd from the window of the citadel—

2.L. How deep?

ar. Thirty fathom.

.L. Three great oaths would scarce make that be believed.

ar. I would I had any drum of the enemy's : I would
    swear I recover'd it.   60

.L. You shall hear one anon.

ar. A drum now of the enemy's,—   *Alarum within*

.L. Throca movousus, cargo, cargo, cargo.

All. Cargo, cargo, cargo, villianda par corbo, cargo.

ar. O, ransom, ransom ! do not hide mine eyes.

        They seize and blindfold him

.S. Boskos thromuldo boskos.

ar. I know you are the Muskos' regiment :
    And I shall lose my life for want of language :
    If there be here German, or Dane, low Dutch,
    Italian, or French, let him speak to me ; I 'll   70
    Discover that which shall undo the Florentine.

.S. Boskos vauvado : I understand thee, and can speak
    thy tongue. Kerelybonto, sir, betake thee to thy
    faith, for seventeen poniards are at thy bosom.

ar. O !

.S. O, pray, pray, pray ! Manka revania dulche.

.L. Oscorbidulchos volivorco.

.S. The general is content to spare thee yet ;
    And, hoodwink'd as thou art, will lead thee on
    To gather from thee : haply thou mayst inform   80

Something to save thy life.

Par.   O, let me live !
And all the secrets of our camp I'll show,
Their force, their purposes ; nay, I'll speak that
Which you will wonder at.

1.*S.*   But wilt thou faithfully ?

Par. If I do not, damn me.

1.*S.* Acordo linta.
Come on, thou art granted space.

    Exit with Parolles guarded.   A short alarum within

2.*L.* Go, tell the count Rossillion and my brother,
We have caught the woodcock, and will keep him
    muffled
Till we do hear from them.

2.*S.*   Captain, I will.   9

2.*L.* A' will betray us all unto ourselves :
Inform on that.

2.*S.* So I will, sir.

2.*L.* Till then I'll keep him dark and safely lock'd.

                                        Exeunt

SCENE II

Florence.   The Widow's house

Enter Bertram and Diana

Ber. They told me that your name was Fontibell.

Dia. No, my good lord, Diana.

Ber.   Titled goddess ;
    And worth it with addition !   But, fair soul,
    In your fine frame hath love no quality ?
    If the quick fire of youth light not your mind,
    You are no maiden, but a monument :
    When you are dead, you should be such a one
    As you are now, for you are cold and stern ;
    And now you should be as your mother was
    When your sweet self was got.   10

Dia. She then was honest.

Ber.   So should you be.

Dia.   No :
    My mother did but duty ; such, my lord,
    As you owe to your wife.

Ber.   No more o' that ;
    I prithee, do not strive against my vows :
    I was compell'd to her, but I love thee
    By love's own sweet constraint, and will for ever

    Do thee all rights of service.

Dia.   Ay, so you serve us
    Till we serve you ; but when you have our roses,
    You barely leave our thorns to prick ourselves,
    And mock us with our bareness.

Ber.   How have I sworn !   20

Dia. 'Tis not the many oaths that makes the truth,
    But the plain single vow that is vow'd true.
    What is not holy, that we swear not by,
    But take the High'st to witness : then, pray, you tell me,
    If I should swear by Jove's great attributes,
    I lov'd you dearly, would you believe my oaths,
    When I did love you ill ?   This has no holding,
    To swear by him whom I protest to love,
    That I will work against him : therefore your oaths
    Are words and poor, conditions but unseal'd,   †
    At least in my opinion.

Ber.   Change it, change it ;   31
    Be not so holy-cruel : love is holy,
    And my integrity ne'er knew the crafts
    That you do charge men with.   Stand no more off,
    But give thyself unto my sick desires,
    Who then recovers : say thou art mine, and ever
    My love, as it begins, shall so persever.

Dia. I see that men make rope's in such a scarre   †

That we 'll forsake ourselves.   Give me that ring.

Ber. I 'll lend it thee, my dear ; but have no power   40
　　To give it from me.

Dia.　　　　　　　　Will you not, my lord ?

Ber. It is an honour 'longing to our house,
　　Bequeathed down from many ancestors,
　　Which were the greatest obloquy i' the world
　　In me to lose.

Dia.　　　　　Mine honour 's such a ring :
　　My chastity 's the jewel of our house,
　　Bequeathed down from many ancestors,
　　Which were the greatest obloquy i' the world
　　In me to lose : thus your own proper wisdom
　　Brings in the champion Honour on my part,   50
　　Against your vain assault.

Ber.　　　　　　　　　　Here, take my ring :
　　My house, mine honour, yea, my life, be thine,
　　And I 'll be bid by thee.

Dia. When midnight comes, knock at my chamber-window :
　　I 'll order take my mother shall not hear.
　　Now will I charge you in the band of truth,
　　When you have conquer'd my yet maiden bed,
　　Remain there but an hour, nor speak to me :
　　My reasons are most strong ; and you shall know them
　　When back again this ring shall be deliver'd :   60

And on your finger in the night I'll put
Another ring, that what in time proceeds
May token to the future our past deeds.
Adieu till then, then fail not. You have won
A wife of me, though there my hope be done.

Ber. A heaven on earth I have won by wooing thee. *Exit*
Dia. For which live long to thank both heaven and me!
You may so in the end.
My mother told me just how he would woo,
As if she sat in's heart; she says all men   70
Have the like oaths: he had sworn to marry me
When his wife's dead; therefore I'll lie with him
When I am buried. Since Frenchmen are so braid, †
Marry that will, I live and die a maid:
Only in this disguise I think 't no sin
To cozen him that would unjustly win.   *Exit*

SCENE III

The Florentine camp

Enter the two French Lords and some two or three Soldiers

1.*L.* You have not given him his mother's letter?
2.*L.* I have deliver'd it an hour since: there is something
     in 't that stings his nature; for on the reading it he
     chang'd almost into another man.

88

1.*L.* He has much worthy blame laid upon him for
shaking off so good a wife and so sweet a lady.

2.*L.* Especially he hath incurred the everlasting displeasure of the king, who had even tun'd his bounty
to sing happiness to him. I will tell you a thing,
but you shall let it dwell darkly with you.   10

1.*L.* When you have spoken it, 'tis dead, and I am the
grave of it.

2.*L.* He hath perverted a young gentlewoman here in
Florence, of a most chaste renown, and this night
he fleshes his will in the spoil of her honour: he
hath given her his monumental ring, and thinks
himself made in the unchaste composition.

1.*L.* Now, God delay our rebellion! as we are ourselves,
what things are we!

2.*L.* Merely our own traitors. And as in the common 20
course of all treasons, we still see them reveal themselves, till they attain to their abhorr'd ends, so he
that in this action contrives against his own nobility,
in his proper stream o'erflows himself.

1.*L.* Is it not meant damnable in us, to be trumpeters
of our unlawful intents? We shall not then have
his company to-night?

2.*L.* Not till after midnight; for he is dieted to his hour.

1.*L.* That approaches apace: I would gladly have him

see his company anatomiz'd, that he might take a   30
measure of his own judgements, wherein so curiously
he had set this counterfeit.

2.*L.* We will not meddle with him till he come ; for his
presence must be the whip of the other.

1.*L.* In the mean time, what hear you of these wars ?

2.*L.* I hear there is an overture of peace.

1.*L.* Nay, I assure you, a peace concluded.

2.*L.* What will Count Rossillion do then ? will he travel
higher, or return again into France ?

1.*L.* I perceive, by this demand, you are not altogether   40
of his council.

2.*L.* Let it be forbid, sir ; so should I be a great deal of
his act.

1.*L.* Sir, his wife some two months since fled from his
house : her pretence is a pilgrimage to Saint Jaques
le Grand ; which holy undertaking with most austere
sanctimony she accomplish'd ; and, there residing,
the tenderness of her nature became as a prey to
her grief ; in fine, made a groan of her last breath,
and now she sings in heaven.   50

2.*L.* How is this justified ?

1.*L.* The stronger part of it by her own letters, which
makes her story true, even to the point of her death :
her death itself, which could not be her office to

say is come, was faithfully confirmed by the rector
of the place.

2.L. Hath the count all this intelligence?

1.L. Ay, and the particular confirmations, point from
point, to the full arming of the verity.

2.L. I am heartily sorry that he'll be glad of this.   60

1.L. How mightly sometimes we make us comforts
of our losses!

2.L. And how mightily some other times we drown our
gain in tears! The great dignity that his valour
hath here acquir'd for him shall at home be encounter'd with a shame as ample.

1.L. The web of our life is of a mingled yarn, good and ill
together: our virtues would be proud, if our faults
whipped them not; and our crimes would despair, if
they were not cherished by our virtues.   70

Enter a Messenger

How now? where's your master?

Ser. He met the Duke in the street, sir, of whom he hath
taken a solemn leave: his lordship will next morning
for France. The Duke hath offered him letters of
commendations to the king.

2.L. They shall be no more than needful there, if they
were more than they can commend.

1.*L.* They cannot be too sweet for the king's tartness.
Here's his lordship now.

Enter Bertram

How now, my lord, is 't not after midnight?   80

Ber. I have to-night dispatch'd sixteen businesses, a
month's length a-piece, by an abstract of success : I †
have congied with the Duke, done my adieu with his
nearest ; buried a wife, mourn'd for her, writ to my
lady mother I am returning, entertain'd my convoy,
and between these main parcels of dispatch effected
many nicer needs : the last was the greatest, but that I
have not ended yet.

2.*L.* If the business be of any difficulty, and this morning
your departure hence, it requires haste of your   90
lordship.

Ber. I mean, the business is not ended, as fearing to hear
of it hereafter.   But shall we have this dialogue
between the fool and the soldier ?   Come, bring
forth this counterfeit module, has deceived me, like
a double-meaning prophesier.

2.*L.* Bring him forth : has sat i' the stocks all night, poor
gallant knave.

Ber. No matter ; his heels have deserv'd it, in usurping
his spurs so long.   How does he carry himself ?   100

2.*L.* I have told your lordship already, the stocks carry

him. But to answer you as you would be understood,
he weeps like a wench that had shed her milk, he hath
confess'd himself to Morgan, whom he supposes to
be a friar, from the time of his remembrance to this
very instant disaster of his setting i' the stocks : and
what think you he hath confessed ?

Ber. Nothing of me, has a' ?

2.L. His confession is taken, and it shall be read to his
face : if your lordship be in 't, as I believe you are,   110
you must have the patience to hear it.

Enter Parolles guarded, and First Soldier

Ber. A plague upon him ! muffled ! he can say nothing of
me : hush, hush !

1.L. Hoodman comes !   Portotartarossa.

1.S. He calls for the tortures : what will you say without
'em ?

Par. I will confess what I know without constraint ; if
ye pinch me like a pasty, I can say no more.

1.S. Bosko chimurcho.

1.L. Boblibindo chicurmurco.   120

1.S. You are a merciful general.   Our general bids you
answer to what I shall ask you out of a note.

Par. And truly, as I hope to live.

1.S. (*reads*) First demand of him how many horse the Duke
is strong.   What say you to that ?

93

Par. Five or six thousand, but very weak and unservice-
    able: the troops are all scattered, and the commanders
    very poor rogues, upon my reputation and credit,
    and as I hope to live.

1.S. Shall I set down your answer so ?   130

Par. Do : I'll take the sacrament on 't, how and which
    way you will.

Ber. All's one to him. What a past-saving slave is this !

1.L. You're deceived, my lord, this is Monsieur Parolles,
    the gallant militarist,—that was his own phrase,—
    that had the whole theoric of war in the knot of his
    scarf, and the practice in the chape of his dagger.

2.L. I will never trust a man again for keeping his sword
    clean, nor believe he can have every thing in him by
    wearing his apparel neatly.   140

1.S. Well, that's set down.

Par. Five or six thousand horse, I said,—I will say true,—
    or thereabouts, set down, for I'll speak truth.

1.L. He's very near the truth in this.

Ber. But I con him no thanks for 't, in the nature he
    delivers it.

Par. Poor rogues, I pray you, say.

1.S. Well, that's set down.

Par. I humbly thank you, sir : a truth's a truth, the rogues
    are marvellous poor.   150

1.*S.* (*reads*) Demand of him, of what strength they are a-foot. What say you to that?

Par. By my troth, sir, if I were to leave this present hour, I will tell true. Let me see : Spurio, a hundred and fifty ; Sebastian, so many ; Corambus, so many ; Jaques, so many ; Guiltian, Cosmo, Lodowick, and Gratii, two hundred fifty each ; mine own company, Chitopher, Vaumond, Bentii, two hundred fifty each : so that the muster-file, rotten and sound, upon my life, amounts not to fifteen thousand poll ; half of the 160 which dare not shake the snow from off their cassocks, lest they shake themselves to pieces.

Ber. What shall be done to him?

1.*L.* Nothing, but let him have thanks. Demand of him my condition, and what credit I have with the Duke.

1.*S.* Well, that's set down. (*reads*) You shall demand of him, whether one Captain Dumain be i' the camp, a Frenchman ; what his reputation is with the Duke, what his valour, honesty, and expertness in wars ; or whether he thinks it were not possible with well- 170 weighing sums of gold to corrupt him to a revolt. What say you to this ; what do you know of it?

Par. I beseech you, let me answer to the particular of the inter'gatories : demand them singly.

1.*S.* Do you know this Captain Dumain?

Par. I know him : a' was a botcher's 'prentice in Paris,
from whence he was whipp'd for getting the
shrieve's fool with child,—a dumb innocent, that †
could not say him nay.

Ber. Nay, by your leave, hold your hands, though I know 180
his brains are forfeit to the next tile that falls.

1.S. Well, is this captain in the Duke of Florence's camp ?

Par. Upon my knowledge, he is, and lousy.

1.L. Nay, look not so upon me ; we shall hear of your
lordship anon.

1.S. What is his reputation with the Duke ?

Par. The Duke knows him for no other but a poor officer
of mine, and writ to me this other day to turn him
out o' the band : I think I have his letter in my
pocket.   190

1.S. Marry, we 'll search.

Par. In good sadness, I do not know ; either it is there,
or it is upon a file with the Duke's other letters in
my tent.

1.S. Here 'tis ; here 's a paper : shall I read it to you ?

Par. I do not know if it be it or no.

Ber. Our interpreter does it well.

1.L. Excellently.

1.S. (*reads*) Dian, the count 's a fool, and full of gold,—

Par. That is not the Duke's letter, sir ; that is an advertise- 200

96

ment to a proper maid in Florence, one Diana, to
take heed of the allurement of one Count Rossillion,
a foolish idle boy, but for all that very ruttish : I
pray you, sir, put it up again.

1.S. Nay, I 'll read it first, by your favour.

Par. My meaning in 't, I protest, was very honest in the
behalf of the maid ; for I knew the young count to
be a dangerous and lascivious boy, who is a whale to
virginity and devours up all the fry it finds.

Ber. Damnable both-sides rogue !   210

1.S. (*reads*) When he swears oaths, bid him drop gold,
        and take it ;
    After he scores, he never pays the score :
    Half won is match well made ; match, and well make it :
        He ne'er pays after-debts, take it before ;
    And say a soldier, Dian, told thee this,
    Men are to mell with, boys are not to kiss :
    For count of this, the count 's a fool, I know it,
    Who pays before, but not when he does owe it.
        Thine, as he vow'd to thee in thine ear,

                                PAROLLES.   220

Ber. He shall be whipp'd through the army with this
rhyme in 's forehead.

2.L. This is your devoted friend, sir, the manifold linguist,
and the armipotent soldier.

97

Ber. I could endure any thing before but a cat, and now
he 's a cat to me.

1.S. I perceive, sir, by the general's looks, we shall be
fain to hang you.

Par. My life, sir, in any case : not that I am afraid to
die, but that, my offences being many, I would repent 230
out the remainder of nature : let me live, sir, in a
dungeon, i' the stocks, or any where, so I may live.

1.S. We 'll see what may be done, so you confess freely ;
therefore, once more to this Captain Dumain : you
have answer'd to his reputation with the Duke and
to his valour : what is his honesty ?

Par. He will steal, sir, an egg out of a cloister : for rapes
and ravishments he parallels Nessus : he professes †
not keeping of oaths ; in breaking 'em he is stronger
than Hercules : he will lie, sir, with such volubility, 240
that you would think truth were a fool : drunkenness
is his best virtue, for he will be swine-drunk, and
in his sleep he does little harm, save to his bed-
clothes about him ; but they know his conditions
and lay him in straw. I have but little more to
say, sir, of his honesty : he has every thing that an
honest man should not have ; what an honest man
should have, he has nothing.

1.L. I begin to love him for this.

Ber. For this description of thine honesty ? A pox 250
    upon him for me, he 's more and more a cat.

1.*S.* What say you to his expertness in war ?

Par. Faith, sir, has led the drum before the English †
    tragedians ; to belie him, I will not, and more of
    his soldiership I know not, except, in that country
    he had the honour to be the officer at a place there
    called Mile-end, to instruct for the doubling of files : †
    I would do the man what honour I can, but of this
    I am not certain.

1.*L.* He hath out-villain'd villany so far, that the rarity 260
    redeems him.

Ber. A pox on him, he 's a cat still.

1.*S.* His qualities being at this poor price, I need not to
    ask you if gold will corrupt him to revolt.

Par. Sir, for a cardecue he will sell the fee-simple of his
    salvation, the inheritance of it, and cut the entail
    from all remainders, and a perpetual succession for
    it perpetually.

1.*S.* What 's his brother, the other Captain Dumain ?

2.*L.* Why does he ask him of me ?   270

1.*S.* What 's he ?

Par. E'en a crow o' the same nest ; not altogether so
    great as the first in goodness, but greater a great
    deal in evil : he excels his brother for a coward,

yet his brother is reputed one of the best that is : in
a retreat he outruns any lackey ; marry, in coming
on he has the cramp.

1.S. If your life be saved, will you undertake to betray
the Florentine ?

Par. Ay, and the captain of his horse, Count Rossillion. 280

1.S. I 'll whisper with the general, and know his pleasure.

Par. (*aside*) I 'll no more drumming, a plague of all drums!
Only to seem to deserve well, and to beguile the
supposition of that lascivious young boy the count,
have I run into this danger.   Yet who would have
suspected an ambush where I was taken ?

1.S. There is no remedy, sir, but you must die : the
general says, you that have so traitorously discover'd
the secrets of your army and made such pestiferous
reports of men very nobly held, can serve the world 290
for no honest use ; therefore you must die.   Come,
headsman, off with his head.

Par. O Lord, sir, let me live, or let me see my death !

1.S. That shall you, and take your leave of all your friends.

Unblinding him

So, look about you : know you any here ?

Ber. Good morrow, noble captain.

2.L. God bless you, Captain Parolles.

1.L. God save you, noble captain.

2.*L.* Captain, what greeting will you to my Lord Lafeu?
     I am for France.   300

1.*L.* Good captain, will you give me a copy of the sonnet
     you writ to Diana in behalf of the Count Rossillion?
     an I were not a very coward, I 'ld compel it of you:
     but fare you well.   *Exeunt Bertram and Lords*

1.*S.* You are undone, captain, all but your scarf; that
     has a knot on 't yet.

Par. Who cannot be crush'd with a plot?

1.*S.* If you could find out a country where but women
     were that had received so much shame, you might
     begin an impudent nation.   Fare ye well, sir; I am 310
     for France too: we shall speak of you there.
                                Exit with Soldiers

Par. Yet am I thankful: if my heart were great,
     'Twould burst at this. Captain I 'll be no more;
     But I will eat and drink, and sleep as soft
     As captain shall: simply the thing I am
     Shall make me live. Who knows himself a braggart,
     Let him fear this, for it will come to pass
     That every braggart shall be found an ass.
     Rust, sword! cool, blushes! and, Parolles, live
     Safest in shame! being fool'd, by foolery thrive! 320
     There 's place and means for every man alive.
     I 'll after them.   *Exit*

SCENE IV

Florence.   The Widow's house

Enter Helena, Widow, and Diana

Hel. That you may well perceive I have not wrong'd you,
One of the greatest in the Christian world
Shall be my surety ; 'fore whose throne 'tis needful,
Ere I can perfect mine intents, to kneel :
Time was, I did him a desired office,
Dear almost as his life, which gratitude
Through flinty Tartar's bosom would peep forth,
And answer thanks : I duly am inform'd
His Grace is at Marseilles ; to which place
We have convenient convoy. You must know,   10
I am supposed dead : the army breaking,
My husband hies him home ; where, heaven aiding
And by the leave of my good lord the king,
We 'll be before our welcome.

Wid.   Gentle madam,
You never had a servant to whose trust
Your business was more welcome.

Hel.   Nor you, mistress,
Ever a friend whose thoughts more truly labour
To recompense your love : doubt not but heaven

Hath brought me up to be your daughter's dower,
As it hath fated her to be my motive   20
And helper to a husband.   But, O strange men !
That can such sweet use make of what they hate,
When saucy trusting of the cozen'd thoughts
Defiles the pitchy night : so lust doth play
With what it loathes for that which is away.
But more of this hereafter.   You, Diana,
Under my poor instructions yet must suffer
Something in my behalf.

Dia.   Let death and honesty
Go with your impositions, I am yours
Upon your will to suffer.

Hel.   Yet, I pray you :   30
But with the word that time will bring on summer,
When briers shall have leaves as well as thorns,
And be as sweet as sharp.   We must away ;
Our waggon is prepar'd, and time revives us :
ALL 'S WELL THAT ENDS WELL : still the fine 's the
    crown ;
Whate'er the course, the end is the renown.   *Exeunt*

SCENE V

Rossillion.   The Count's palace

Enter Countess, Lafeu, and Clown

Laf. No, no, no, your son was misled with a snipt-taffeta
fellow there, whose villanous saffron would have
made all the unbak'd and doughy youth of a nation
in his colour : your daughter-in-law had been alive at
this hour, and your son here at home, more advanc'd
by the king than by that red-tail'd humble-bee I
speak of.

Cou. I would I had not known him ; it was the death of
the most virtuous gentlewoman that ever nature had
praise for creating.   If she had partaken of my   10
flesh, and cost me the dearest groans of a mother,
I could not have owed her a more rooted love.

Laf. 'Twas a good lady, 'twas a good lady : we may pick
a thousand salads ere we light on such another herb.

Clo. Indeed, sir, she was the sweet-marjoram of the salad,
or rather, the herb of grace.

Laf. They are knot herbs, you knave ; they are nose-herbs. †

Clo. I am no great Nebuchadnezzar, sir ; I have not much
skill in grass.

Laf. Whether dost thou profess thyself, a knave or a fool ?   20

Clo. A fool, sir, at a woman's service, and a knave at a man's.

Laf. Your distinction ?

Clo. I would cozen the man of his wife and do his service.

Laf. So you were a knave at his service, indeed.

Clo. And I would give his wife my bauble, sir, to do her service.

Laf. I will subscribe for thee, thou art both knave and fool.

Clo. At your service.   30

Laf. No, no, no.

Clo. Why, sir, if I cannot serve you, I can serve as great a prince as you are.

Laf. Who 's that ? a Frenchman ?

Clo. Faith, sir, a' has an English name ; but his fisnamy is more hotter in France than there.

Laf. What prince is that ?

Clo. The black prince, sir, alias the prince of darkness, alias the devil.

Laf. Hold thee, there 's my purse : I give thee not this   40
to suggest thee from thy master thou talkest of ;
serve him still.

Clo. I am a woodland fellow, sir, that always loved a great fire ; and the master I speak of ever keeps a

good fire.   But, sure, he is the prince of the world ;
let his nobility remain in 's court.   I am for the
house with the narrow gate, which I take to be too
little for pomp to enter : some that humble themselves may ; but the many will be too chill and
tender, and they 'll be for the flowery way that   50
leads to the broad gate, and the great fire.

Laf. Go thy ways, I begin to be aweary of thee ; and I
tell thee so before, because I would not fall out with
thee.   Go thy ways, let my horses be well looked
to, without any tricks.

Clo. If I put any tricks upon 'em, sir, they shall be jades'
tricks, which are their own right by the law of nature.

Exit

Laf. A shrewd knave and an unhappy.

Cou. So he is.   My lord that 's gone made himself much
sport out of him : by his authority he remains here,   60
which he thinks is a patent for his sauciness ; and
indeed he has no pace, but runs where he will.

Laf. I like him well, 'tis not amiss.   And I was about to
tell you, since I heard of the good lady's death and
that my lord your son was upon his return home, I
moved the king my master to speak in the behalf of
my daughter ; which, in the minority of them both,
his majesty, out of a self-gracious remembrance, did

first propose : his highness hath promis'd me to do
it : and, to stop up the displeasure he hath conceived   70
against your son, there is no fitter matter.   How
does your ladyship like it ?

Cou. With very much content, my lord, and I wish it
happily effected.

Laf. His highness comes post from Marseilles, of as able
body as when he number'd thirty : he will be here
to-morrow, or I am deceiv'd by him that in such
intelligence hath seldom fail'd.

Cou. It rejoices me, that I hope I shall see him ere I die.
I have letters that my son will be here to-night : I   80
shall beseech your lordship to remain with me till
they meet together.

Laf. Madam, I was thinking with what manners I might
safely be admitted.

Cou. You need but plead your honourable privilege.

Laf. Lady, of that I have made a bold charter, but I thank
my God it holds yet.

Re-enter Clown

Clo. O madam, yonder 's my lord your son with a patch †
of velvet on 's face : whether there be a scar under 't
or no, the velvet knows, but 'tis a goodly patch of   90
velvet : his left cheek is a cheek of two pile and a
half, but his right cheek is worn bare.

Laf. A scar nobly got, or a noble scar, is a good livery of
    honour ; so belike is that.

Clo. But it is your carbonadoed face.

Laf. Let us go see your son, I pray you : I long to talk
    with the young noble soldier.

Clo. Faith, there's a dozen of 'em, with delicate fine hats
    and most courteous feathers, which bow the head
    and nod at every man.   *Exeunt* 100

Act Fifth

SCENE I

Marseilles. A street

Enter Helena, Widow, and Diana, with two Attendants

Hel. But this exceeding posting day and night
    Must wear your spirits low ; we cannot help it :
    But since you have made the days and nights as one,
    To wear your gentle limbs in my affairs,
    Be bold you do so grow in my requital
    As nothing can unroot you.   In happy time :
                            Enter a Gentleman   †
    This man may help me to his majesty's ear,

> If he would spend his power.   God save you, sir.

Gen. And you.

Hel. Sir, I have seen you in the court of France.   10

Gen. I have been sometimes there.

Hel. I do presume, sir, that you are not fallen
> From the report that goes upon your goodness ;
> And therefore, goaded with most sharp occasions,
> Which lay nice manners by, I put you to
> The use of your own virtues, for the which
> I shall continue thankful.

Gen.   What 's your will ?

Hel. That it will please you
> To give this poor petition to the king,
> And aid me with that store of power you have   20
> To come into his presence.

Gen. The king 's not here.

Hel.   Not here, sir ?

Gen.   Not, indeed :
> He hence remov'd last night and with more haste
> Than is his use.

Wid.   Lord, how we lose our pains !

Hel. ALL 'S WELL THAT ENDS WELL yet,
> Though time seem so adverse, and means unfit.
> I do beseech you, whither is he gone ?

Gen. Marry, as I take it, to Rossillion ;

Whither I am going.

Hel.   I do beseech you, sir,
Since you are like to see the king before me,   30
Commend the paper to his gracious hand,
Which I presume shall render you no blame,
But rather make you thank your pains for it.
I will come after you with what good speed
Our means will make us means.

Gen.   This I 'll do for you.

Hel. And you shall find yourself to be well thank'd,
Whate'er falls more.   We must to horse again.
Go, go, provide.   *Exeunt*

SCENE II

Rossillion.   Before the Count's palace

Enter Clown, and Parolles, following

Par. Good Monsieur Lavache, give my Lord Lafeu this
letter : I have ere now, sir, been better known to you,
when I have held familiarity with fresher clothes ;
but I am now, sir, muddied in fortune's mood, and
smell somewhat strong of her strong displeasure.

Clo. Truly, fortune's displeasure is but sluttish, if it smell
so strongly as thou speakest of : I will henceforth

eat no fish of fortune's buttering. Prithee, allow
the wind.

Par. Nay, you need not to stop your nose, sir ; I spake but   10
    by a metaphor.

Clo. Indeed, sir, if your metaphor stink, I will stop my
    nose, or against any man's metaphor. Prithee, get
    thee further.

Par. Pray you, sir, deliver me this paper.

Clo. Foh ! prithee, stand away : a paper from fortune's
    close-stool to give to a nobleman ! Look, here he
    comes himself.

Enter Lafeu

Here is a pur of fortune's, sir, or of fortune's cat,—   †
but not a musk-cat,—that has fallen into the unclean   20
fishpond of her displeasure, and, as he says, is
muddied withal : pray you, sir, use the carp as you
may ; for he looks like a poor, decayed, ingenious,
foolish, rascally knave. I do pity his distress in my
similes of comfort and leave him to your lordship.

Exit

Par. My lord, I am a man whom fortune hath cruelly
    scratch'd.

Laf. And what would you have me to do ? 'Tis too late
    to pare her nails now. Wherein have you play'd
    the knave with fortune, that she should scratch   30

you, who of herself is a good lady and would not
have knaves thrive long- under her? There 's a
cardecu for you : let the justices make you and
fortune friends : I am for other business.

Par. I beseech your honour to hear me one single word.

Laf. You beg a single penny more : come, you shall ha 't ;
save your word.

Par. My name, my good lord, is Parolles.

Laf. You beg more than ' word,' then.   Cox my passion !
give me your hand.   How does your drum !   40

Par. O my good lord, you were the first that found me !

Laf. Was I, in sooth ? and I was the first that lost thee.

Par. It lies in you, my lord, to bring me in some grace,
for you did bring me out.

Laf. Out upon thee, knave ! dost thou put upon me at
once both the office of God and the devil ?   One
brings thee in grace and the other brings thee out.
(*Trumpets sound.*)   The king 's coming ; I know by
his trumpets.   Sirrah, inquire further after me ; I
had talk of you last night : though you are a fool   50
and a knave, you shall eat ; go to, follow.

Par. I praise God for you.   *Exeunt*

SCENE III

Rossillion.   The Count's palace

Flourish.   Enter King, Countess, Lafeu, the two French Lords, with Attendants

King. We lost a jewel of her, and our esteem
    Was made much poorer by it : but your son,
    As mad in folly, lack'd the sense to know
    Her estimation home.

Cou.   'Tis past, my liege ;
    And I beseech your majesty to make it
    Natural rebellion, done i' the blaze of youth ;
    When oil and fire, too strong for reason's force,
    O'erbears it, and burns on.

King.   My honour'd lady,
    I have forgiven and forgotten all ;
    Though my revenges were high bent upon him,   10
    And watch'd the time to shoot.

Laf.   This I must say,
    But first I beg my pardon, the young lord
    Did to his majesty, his mother and his lady
    Offence of mighty note ; but to himself
    The greatest wrong of all.   He lost a wife
    Whose beauty did astonish the survey

Of richest eyes, whose words all ears took captive,
Whose dear perfection hearts that scorn'd to serve
Humbly call'd mistress.

King.   Praising what is lost
Makes the remembrance dear. Well, call him hither; 20
We are reconcil'd, and the first view shall kill
All repetition: let him not ask our pardon;
The nature of his great offence is dead,
And deeper than oblivion we do bury
The incensing relics of it: let him approach,
A stranger, no offender; and inform him
So 'tis our will he should.

Gen.   I shall, my liege.   *Exit*

King. What says he to your daughter? have you spoke?

Laf. All that he is hath reference to your highness.

King. Then shall we have a match. I have letters sent me 30
That set him high in fame.

Enter Bertram

Laf.   He looks well on't.

King. I am not a day of season,
For thou mayst see a sunshine and a hail
In me at once: but to the brightest beams
Distracted clouds give way; so stand thou forth;
The time is fair again.

Ber.   My high-repented blames,

Dear sovereign, pardon to me.

King.   All is whole ;

Not one word more of the consumed time.
Let's take the instant by the forward top ;
For we are old, and on our quick'st decrees   40
The inaudible and noiseless foot of Time
Steals, ere we can effect them.   You remember
The daughter of this lord ?

Ber. Admiringly, my liege, at first
I stuck my choice upon her, ere my heart
Durst make too bold a herald of my tongue :
Where the impression of mine eye infixing,
Contempt his scornful perspective did lend me,
Which warp'd the line of every other favour ;
Scorn'd a fair colour, or express'd it stolen ;   50
Extended or contracted all proportions
To a most hideous object : thence it came
That she whom all men prais'd and whom myself,
Since I have lost, have lov'd, was in mine eye
The dust that did offend it.

King.   Well excus'd :

That thou didst love her, strikes some scores away
From the great compt : but love that comes too late,
Like a remorseful pardon slowly carried
To the great sender, turns a sour offence,

Crying ' That's good that's gone.'   Our rash faults   60
Make trivial price of serious things we have,
Not knowing them until we know their grave :
Oft our displeasures, to ourselves unjust,
Destroy our friends, and after weep their dust :
Our own love waking cries to see what's done,
While shameful hate sleeps out the afternoon.
Be this sweet Helen's knell, and now forget her.
Send forth your amorous token for fair Maudlin :
The main consents are had, and here we'll stay
To see our widower's second marriage-day.   70

Cou. Which better than the first, O dear heaven, bless !
Or, ere they meet, in me, O nature, cesse !

Laf. Come on, my son, in whom my house's name
Must be digested, give a favour from you
To sparkle in the spirits of my daughter,
That she may quickly come.   (*Bertram gives a ring.*)
      By my old beard,
And every hair that's on't, Helen, that's dead,
Was a sweet creature : such a ring as this,
The last time e'er I took her leave at court,
I saw upon her finger.

Ber.   Hers it was not.   80

King. Now, pray you, let me see it ; for mine eye,
While I was speaking, oft was fasten'd to't.

This ring was mine ; and, when I gave it Helen,
I bade her, if her fortunes ever stood
Necessitied to help, that by this token
I would relieve her.   Had you that craft, to reave her
Of what should stead her most ?

Ber.   My gracious sovereign,
Howe'er it pleases you to take it so,
The ring was never hers.

Cou.   Son, on my life,
I have seen her wear it, and she reckon'd it   90
At her life's rate.

Laf.   I am sure I saw her wear it.

Ber. You are deceiv'd, my lord ; she never saw it :
In Florence was it from a casement thrown me,
Wrapp'd in a paper, which contain'd the name
Of her that threw it : noble she was, and thought
I stood ungag'd : but when I had subscrib'd
To mine own fortune and inform'd her fully
I could not answer in that course of honour
As she had made the overture, she ceas'd
In heavy satisfaction, and would never   100
Receive the ring again.

King.   Plutus himself,
That knows the tinct and multiplying medicine,
Hath not in nature's mystery more science

    Than I have in this ring : 'twas mine, 'twas Helen's,
    Whoever gave it you.   Then, if you know
    That you are well acquainted with yourself,
    Confess 'twas hers, and by what rough enforcement
    You got it from her : she call'd the saints to surety
    That she would never put it from her finger,
    Unless she gave it to yourself in bed,   110
    Where you have never come, or sent it us
    Upon her great disaster.

Ber.   She never saw it.

*King.*Thou speak'st it falsely, as I love mine honour ;
    And makest conjectural fears to come into me,
    Which I would fain shut out.   If it should prove
    That thou art so inhuman,—'twill not prove so ;—
    And yet I know not : thou didst hate her deadly,
    And she is dead ; which nothing, but to close
    Her eyes myself, could win me to believe,
    More than to see this ring.   Take him away.   120

                     Guards seize Bertram

    My fore-past proofs, howe'er the matter fall,
    Shall tax my fears of little vanity,
    Having vainly fear'd too little.   Away with him !
    We'll sift this matter further.

Ber.   If you shall prove
    This ring was ever hers, you shall as easy

Prove that I husbanded her bed in Florence,
Where yet she never was.   *Exit, guarded*

*King.*I am wrapp'd in dismal thinkings.

Enter a Gentleman

Gen.   Gracious sovereign,
Whether I have been to blame or no, I know not :
Here 's a petition from a Florentine,   130
Who hath for four or five removes come short
To tender it herself.   I undertook it,
Vanquish'd thereto by the fair grace and speech
Of the poor suppliant, who by this I know
Is here attending : her business looks in her
With an importing visage ; and she told me,
In a sweet verbal brief, it did concern
Your highness with herself.

King.(reads) Upon his many protestations to marry me
when his wife was dead, I blush to say it, he won me.   140
Now is the Count Rossillion a widower, his vows
are forfeited to me, and my honour 's paid to him.
He stole from Florence, taking no leave, and I follow
him to his country for justice : grant it me, O king !
in you it best lies ; otherwise a seducer flourishes,
and a poor maid is undone.   DIANA CAPILET.

Laf. I will buy me a son-in-law in a fair, and toll for this :
I 'll none of him.

119

King. The heavens have thought well on thee, Lafeu,
    To bring forth this discovery.   Seek these suitors :   150
    Go speedily and bring again the count.
    I am afeard the life of Helen, lady,
    Was foully snatch'd.

Cou.   Now, justice on the doers !

Re-enter Bertram, guarded

King. I wonder, sir, sith wives are monsters to you,
    And that you fly them as you swear them lordship,
    Yet you desire to marry.

Enter Widow and Diana

                 What woman 's that ?

Dia. I am, my lord, a wretched Florentine,
    Derived from the ancient Capilet :
    My suit, as I do understand, you know,
    And therefore know how far I may be pitied.   160

Wid. I am her mother, sir, whose age and honour
    Both suffer under this complaint we bring,
    And both shall cease, without your remedy.

King. Come hither, count ; do you know these women ?

Ber. My lord, I neither can nor will deny
    But that I know them : do they charge me further ?

Dia. Why do you look so strange upon your wife ?

Ber. She 's none of mine, my lord.

Dia.   If you shall marry,

You give away this hand, and that is mine ;
You give away heaven's vows, and those are mine ;   170
You give away myself, which is known mine ;
For I by vow am so embodied yours,
That she which marries you must marry me,
Either both or none.

Laf. Your reputation comes too short for my daughter ;
  you are no husband for her.

Ber. My lord, this is a fond and desperate creature,
  Whom sometime I have laugh'd with : let your
    highness
  Lay a more noble thought upon mine honour
  Than for to think that I would sink it here.   180

*King.*Sir, for my thoughts, you have them ill to friend
  Till your deeds gain them : fairer prove your honour
  Than in my thought it lies.

Dia.   Good my lord,
  Ask him upon his oath, if he does think
  He had not my virginity.

*King.*What say'st thou to her ?

Ber.   She 's impudent, my lord,
  And was a common gamester to the camp.

Dia. He does me wrong, my lord ; if I were so,
  He might have bought me at a common price :
  Do not believe him.   O, behold this ring,   190

       Whose high respect and rich validity
       Did lack a parallel ; yet for all that
       He gave it to a commoner o' the camp,
       If I be one.

Cou.   He blushes, and 'tis it :
       Of six preceding ancestors, that gem,
       Conferr'd by testament to the sequent issue,
       Hath it been owed and worn.   This is his wife ;
       That ring 's a thousand proofs.

King.   Methought you said
       You saw one here in court could witness it.

Dia. I did, my lord, but loath am to produce   200
       So bad an instrument : his name 's Parolles.

Laf. I saw the man to-day, if man he be.

King. Find him, and bring him hither.   *Exit an Attendant*

Ber.   What of him ?
       He 's quoted for a most perfidious slave,
       With all the spots o' the world tax'd and debosh'd ;
       Whose nature sickens but to speak a truth.
       Am I or that or this for what he 'll utter,
       That will speak any thing ?

King.   She hath that ring of yours.

Ber. I think she has : certain it is I lik'd her,
       And boarded her i' the wanton way of youth :   210
       She knew her distance, and did angle for me,

Madding my eagerness with her restraint,
As all impediments in fancy's course
Are motives of more fancy, and, in fine,
Her infinite cunning, with her modern grace,
Subdued me to her rate : she got the ring ;
And I had that which any inferior might
At market-price have bought.

Dia.   I must be patient :
You, that have turn'd off a first so noble wife,
May justly diet me.   I pray you yet,   220
(Since you lack virtue I will lose a husband)
Send for your ring, I will return it home,
And give me mine again.

Ber.   I have it not.

King. What ring was yours, I pray you ?

Dia.   Sir, much like
The same upon your finger.

King. Know you this ring ? this ring was his of late.

Dia. And this was it I gave him, being abed.

King. The story then goes false, you threw it him
Out of a casement.

Dia.   I have spoke the truth.

Enter Parolles

Ber. My lord, I do confess the ring was hers.   230

King. You boggle shrewdly, every feather starts you.

123

   Is this the man you speak of?

Dia.   Ay, my lord.

*King.*Tell me, sirrah, but tell me true, I charge you,
   Not fearing the displeasure of your master,
   Which on your just proceeding I'll keep off,
   By him and by this woman here what know you?

Par. So please your majesty, my master hath been an
   honourable gentleman: tricks he hath had in him,
   which gentlemen have.

*King.*Come, come, to the purpose: did he love this 240
   woman?

Par. Faith, sir, he did love her; but how?

*King.*How, I pray you?

Par. He did love her, sir, as a gentleman loves a woman.

*King.*How is that?

Par. He lov'd her, sir, and lov'd her not.

*King.*As thou art a knave, and no knave. What an
   equivocal companion is this!

Par. I am a poor man, and at your majesty's command.

Laf. He's a good drum, my lord, but a naughty orator. 250

Dia. Do you know he promis'd me marriage?

Par. Faith, I know more than I'll speak.

*King.*But wilt thou not speak all thou knowest?

Par. Yes, so please your majesty. I did go between them,
   as I said; but more than that he lov'd her, for

indeed he was mad for her, and talk'd of Satan,
and of Limbo, and of Furies, and I know not what:
yet I was in that credit with them at that time, that
I knew of their going to bed, and of other motions,
as promising her marriage, and things which would   260
derive me ill will to speak of; therefore I will not
speak what I know.

*King.*Thou hast spoken all already, unless thou canst say
they are married, but thou art too fine in thy evidence, therefore stand aside.

This ring, you say, was yours?

Dia.   Ay, my good lord.

*King.*Where did you buy it? or who gave it you?

Dia. It was not given me, nor I did not buy it.

*King.*Who lent it you?

Dia.   It was not lent me neither.

*King.*Where did you find it then?

Dia.   I found it not.   270

*King.*If it were yours by none of all these ways,
How could you give it him?

Dia.   I never gave it him.

Laf. This woman's an easy glove, my lord; she goes off
and on at pleasure.

*King.*This ring was mine; I gave it his first wife.

Dia. It might be yours or hers, for aught I know.

*King.*Take her away ; I do not like her now ;
To prison with her : and away with him.
Unless thou tell'st me where thou hadst this ring,
Thou diest within this hour.

Dia.   I 'll never tell you.   280

*King.*Take her away.

Dia.   I 'll put in bail, my liege.

*King.*I think thee now some common customer.

Dia. By Jove, if ever I knew man, 'twas you.

*King.*Wherefore hast thou accus'd him all this while ?

Dia. Because he 's guilty, and he is not guilty :
He knows I am no maid, and he 'll swear to 't ;
I 'll swear I am a maid, and he knows not.
Great king, I am no strumpet, by my life ;
I am either maid, or else this old man's wife.

*King.*She does abuse our ears : to prison with her.   290

Dia. Good mother, fetch my bail.   Stay, royal sir :

                                              Exit Widow

The jeweller that owes the ring is sent for,
And he shall surety me.   But for this lord,
Who hath abus'd me, as he knows himself,
Though yet he never harm'd me, here I quit him :
He knows himself my bed he hath defil'd ;
And at that time he got his wife with child :
Dead though she be, she feels her young one kick :

126

So there's my riddle,—One that's dead is quick :
And now behold the meaning.

Re-enter Widow, with Helena

King.   Is there no exorcist   300
    Beguiles the truer office of mine eyes ?
    Is 't real that I see ?

Hel.   No, my good lord ;
    'Tis but the shadow of a wife you see,
    The name and not the thing.

Ber.   Both, both.   O, pardon !

Hel. O good lord, when I was like this maid,
    I found you wondrous kind.   There is your ring ;
    And, look you, here's your letter ; this it says :
    ' When from my finger you can get this ring
    And are by me with child,' &c.   This is done :
    Will you be mine, now you are doubly won ?   310

Ber. If she, my liege, can make me know this clearly,
    I 'll love her dearly, ever, ever dearly.

Hel. If it appear not plain and prove untrue,
    Deadly divorce step between me and you !
    O my dear mother, do I see you living ?

Laf. Mine eyes smell onions ; I shall weep anon :
    (*to Parolles*) Good Tom Drum, lend me a hand-
        kercher : so,

127

> I thank thee : wait on me home, I 'll make sport
>   with thee :
> Let thy courtesies alone, they are scurvy ones.

King. Let us from point to point this story know,   320
> To make the even truth in pleasure flow.
> (*to Diana*) If thou be'st yet a fresh uncropped flower,
> Choose thou thy husband, and I 'll pay thy dower ;
> For I can guess that by thy honest aid
> Thou kept'st a wife herself, thyself a maid.
> Of that and all the progress, more and less,
> Resolvedly more leisure shall express :
> All yet seems well ; and if it end so meet,
> The bitter past, more welcome is the sweet.

Flourish

EPILOGUE

King. The king 's a beggar, now the play is done :
> All is well ended, if this suit be won,
> That you express content ; which we will pay,
> With strife to please you, day exceeding day :
> Ours be your patience then, and yours our parts ;
> Your gentle hands lend us, and take our hearts.

Exeunt

Notes

I. i. 5. *ward*; 'During infancy (*i.e.* up to the ages of twenty-one and sixteen respectively for males and females) the guardian had the right of marrying the ward to anyone he pleased of equal rank.' Though the king does not observe the equality of rank the point is of importance for the plot.

I. i. 56. The New Cambridge editors would put this remark in as the opening of the preceding speech of the Countess, which greatly improves the run of the text.

I. i. 102. *Cold wisdom* . . .; this apparently means that wisdom is left out in the cold and is the servant of, or inferior to, folly that has superfluity of all it wants.

I. i. 104. *monarch*; perhaps an allusion to 'Monarcho,' a crazy Italian at Elizabeth's court; cf. *Love's Labour's Lost*, IV. i. 100.

I. i. 210. *none*; should perhaps be *money*.

I. ii. 43. *another*; perhaps *a nigher* (Williams).

I. iii. 51. *Charbon* . . . *Poysam*; presumably intended for *Chairbonne* and *Poisson*, with allusion to the observance and non-observance of fast-days, with fish or good flesh.

I. iii. 78. *one good in ten*; the song actually said 'one bad in ten'; hence *corrupt the song*.

I. iii. 91. *surplice* . . . *black gown*; the conforming Puritan clergy obeyed the law by wearing the Papistical surplice, but salved their consciences by wearing the Genevan black gown under it.

I. iii. 110. There is clearly an omission. Perhaps *Dian no queen of* . . . . . (Theobald).

I. iii. 198. *intenible*; F reads *intemible*. The New Cambridge editors spend some thirty lines in justifying with erudition and ingenuity their 'normalised spelling' *inteemable*; but it is hard to see why one should not rest content with the easy minim-error *intenible*, with the common enough 'active-for-passive' meaning of 'that will not hold what is poured in.'

I. iii. 208. *Wish chastely* . . .; the New Cambridge editors say that the compositor 'obviously' transposed *wish* and *love*, 'thereby making nonsense of the passage'; and think that only cowardice has prevented modern editors from following Malone. A wise cowardice is perhaps not improper in playing fast and loose with the only text we have; nor do I think that F makes nonsense, if we take *that* not after a transposed *wish*, but as meaning *so that*.

I. iii. 221. *In heedfull'st reservation* . . .; either 'put them away with the greatest care,' or 'keep them for use only on the most important occasions.' What the following line and a half means has not been explained, with or without the help of emendations, and I have no suggestion to offer.

I. iii. 238. *in 't*; (?) *hints* (Hanmer).

II. i. 76. *Pepin . . . Charlemain*; ancient kings of France.

II. i. 173. *Sear'd otherwise*; the New Cambridge editors would punctuate with a semicolon after *Sear'd* and no stop after *otherwise*, which is superficially attractive; but it produces an awkward rhythm, and I am not clear that it gives the natural sense, since Helena seems to be considering the various ways in which her maiden name might be 'seared.'

II. iii. 11. *Galen and Paracelsus*; famous physicians, one ancient, one mediæval, of two different schools, the followers of the latter laying particular stress on chemical principles.

II. iii. 25. *dolphin*; one should perhaps read *Dauphin*, for which Dolphin was the ordinary Elizabethan spelling.

II. iii. 77. *than throw ames-ace* . . .; *ames-ace*, or 'ambs-ace,' was the lowest throw at dice. The phrase then seems to be the equivalent of 'that's better than a poke in the eye with a burnt stick.'

II. iii. 84. *Love*; (?) *Jove*.

II. iii. 287. *detested*; an amusing typographical point. F reads *detected*, but as both *st* and *ct* were 'ligatures' there was always a danger of 'foul case.'

II. iv. 33. *find me? The search . . .*; between *find me?* and *The search* Nicholson boldly inserts two words of Parolles, *In myself*. They at least simplify the sense, which must otherwise be deduced.

III. ii. 13. *old lings*; since (see New Cambridge) 'old ling' is salted cod, 'salt' is lecherous, and 'cod' can have the sense it has in 'codpiece,' the general sense of the clown's remarks, if it is worth pursuing, is clear.

III. v. (S.D.). And who is Violenta, what is she? that all the texts include her. She looks like a survival from an earlier state of the play. If she is merely a mistake of the transcriber for Diana why does he give both?

IV. i. 42. *Bajazet's mule*; the New Cambridge editors want to read *Bajazet's mate*, which is indeed an easy enough graphical error, but seems to miss the point. It is true that Zabina was a termagant, but poor Parolles' point is surely exactly the opposite of what the New Cambridge editors take it to be. It is not that to get him *out* of his scrape he wants a scolding tongue; it is that his too fluent tongue gets him *into* scrapes, and so he will give it to a butter-woman who would have a use for it, and get himself a new one that will preserve a discreet silence. Hanmer read *mute*, which would give the required sense, and be acceptable enough if only one knew what the allusion was.

IV. ii. 30. *words and poor, conditions*; the New Cambridge editors punctuate as in the text; F has a comma after *conditions* and none after *poor*. This gives a better sense though an awkward rhythm.

IV. ii. 38. *rope's in such a scarre*; a famous crux. None of the explanations seem to me to carry much conviction. 'Make rapes in such a scour,' for example, though graphically easy, does not seem to give the required sense, which surely is something like ' make such pathetically persuasive pleadings that we yield.'

IV. ii. 73. *braid*; there has been a deal of apparently unnecessary pother about this. It has been explained as 'braided,' *i.e.* plaited, tortuous, or as 'brayed,' *i.e.* damaged. But no one with any acquaintance with Northern speech would ever look further than the straightforward meaning of 'broad,' *i.e.* loose, as the New Cambridge editors point out.

IV. iii. 82. *abstract of success*; usually explained as 'to give a summary of my successes'; but I suspect that it means 'by a brevity of succession,' *i.e.* 'by making each business short and following immediately on its predecessor.'

IV. iii. 178. *shrieve's fool*; 'the sheriff had charge of idiots whose property was not of sufficient value to make them profitable wards for the Crown.'

IV. iii. 238. *Nessus*; the Centaur who ravished Deianira, Heracles' bride.

IV. iii. 253. *led the drum* . . .; *i.e.* 'beaten the drum at the head of the advertising procession through the streets.'

IV. iii. 257. *Mile-end*; where the London train-bands practised their drill.

IV. v. 17. *knot herbs*; the New Cambridge editors most ingeniously suggest this reading for F's *not hearbes*. A 'knot' was a flower-bed, and it is clear that the point is that the herbs are for scent, not taste. The alternative is to fill in, with Rowe and others, and read *not salad-herbs*.

IV. v. 88. It is hardly worth pursuing the elucidation of these tedious syphilitic japes. The disease when it affected the face was dealt with by incision, and the scar covered with velvet plaster.

V. i. 6 (S.D.). F has a mysterious reading, *Enter a gentle Astringer*. An 'astringer' was a kind of falconer, and attempts have been made to give some point to this by assuming that the King had gone to Marseilles for the hawking. But it is surely impossible that an ordinary stage-direction should specify the 'gentleness' of the 'astringer.' I suspect some confusion between an omitted line of Helena's, in which she commented on the fact that the entrant was no stranger to her, and the stage-direction of *Enter a gentleman*.

V. ii. 19. *pur*; in the card game of 'post and pair' the knave was called 'pur.'

Glossary

MANY words and phrases in Shakespeare require glossing, not because they are in themselves unfamiliar, but for the opposite reason, that Shakespeare uses in their Elizabethan and unfamiliar sense a large number of words which seem so familiar that there is no incentive to look for them in the glossary. It is hoped that a glossary arranged as below will make it easy to see at a glance what words and phrases in any particular scene require elucidation. A number of phrases are glossed by what seems to be, in their context, the modern equivalent rather than by lexicographical glosses on the words which compose them.

Act First

SCENE I

line
36 GOOD, *sc. development*
43 FROM HER TEARS, *i.e.* tears from her
44 SEASON, preserve
46 LIVELIHOOD, liveliness
68-69 HE CANNOT WANT THE BEST THAT SHALL ATTEND HIS LORD, he must not be lacking in the best advice who is going to attend on the king
72 COMFORTABLE, comforting
80 FAVOUR, face
85 COLLATERAL, *stars in different spheres moved 'collaterally'*

line
92 TABLE, panel for painting
100 TAKE PLACE, are accepted
108 STAIN, tinge
151 VENDIBLE, marketable
153 SUITED, clothed (*with pun*)
154 WEAR NOT, are not 'the wear'
155 DATE, *i.e.* the fruit, for sweetening
171 ADOPTIOUS CHRISTENDOMS, Christian names of adopted children
172 BLINKING, blind
GOSSIPS, stands godfather to

134

SCENE II

line

3 BRAVING, defiant
9 PREJUDICATES, prejudges
11 APPROV'D, proved
21 CURIOUS, elaborate
29 DISCIPLED, taught by, *or perhaps* followed as a teacher by
41 EXCEPTION, disapproval
47 COPY, pattern

line

51 SO IN APPROOF LIVES NOT, is nowhere so fully confirmed
54 PLAUSIVE, persuasive
60 BE THE SNUFF OF, be snuffed by
61 APPREHENSIVE, quick to apprehend
69 IT, *i.e.* love
75 WITH SEVERAL APPLICATIONS, *i.e.* each with his own cure

SCENE III

41 YOU'RE SHALLOW . . . IN, you know nothing about
43 EARS, ploughs
44 IN, bring in, harvest
53 JOUL, clash
62 KIND, nature
70 FOND, foolishly
115 SITHENCE, since

148 IRIS, rainbow
166 FEAR, suspicion
168 GROSS, plain
178 CLEW, tangle
206 CITES, gives evidence of
226 RENDER'D, pronounced
237 EMBOWELL'D, disembowelled

Act Second

SCENE I

9 OWES, owns
13 BATED, excepted
27 KEPT A-COIL, kept dangling
30 FOREHORSE TO A SMOCK, leader of a team driven by a woman
43 SINISTER, left
50 LIST, limit

52 WEAR THEMSELVES IN THE CAP OF THE TIME, are in the height of fashion
53 MUSTER TRUE GAIT, learn correct carriage
55 MEASURE, dance
56 DILATED, protracted

Act II Sc. i—*continued*

line

61 FEE, pay

72 MEDICINE, doctor

74 CANARY, lively dance

76 ARAISE, resurrect

82 LIGHT DELIVERANCE, casual report

88 ADMIRATION, object of wonder

97 CRESSID'S UNCLE, *i.e.* Pandar

108 TRIPLE, third

113 APPLIANCE, application of it

135 SET UP YOUR REST, are determined

line

150 SQUARE OUR GUESS BY SHOWS, adjust our conjecture by appearances

155-56 PROCLAIM MYSELF AGAINST THE LEVEL OF MINE AIM, promise more than I can perform

162 TORCHER, torch-bearer

183 PRIME, youth

188 PROPERTY, fulfilment

SCENE II

18 QUATCH, *prob.* =quat=fat

22 FRENCH CROWN, *pun on* (*a*) coin, (*b*) baldness caused by syphilis
PUNK, prostitute

23 RUSH, the rush ring used in rustic mock marriages

24 MORRIS, morris-dance

25 HORN, symbol of cuckoldry

27 PUDDING, sausage
HIS, its

51 SEQUENT, following pat

59 PRESENT, immediate

SCENE III

2 MODERN, everyday

12 FELLOWS, *i.e.* of the Royal College of Physicians

28 FACINERIOUS, criminal

33 DEBILE, feeble

42 CORANTO, a quick dance

48 REPEAL'D, recovered

51 PARCEL, batch

54 ELECTION, choice

58 FURNITURE, trappings

138 DEBOSH'D, profaned

149 WHICH, *i.e. the attack on his honour*

152 MISPRISION, despising

159 PRESENTLY, immediately

178 WHOSE, of which

179 SHALL SEEM EXPEDIENT, should rapidly follow

181 ATTEND, wait

183 RELIGIOUS, as in duty bound

190 SUCCEEDING, issue

200 FOR TWO ORDINARIES, for the length of two meals

Act II   Sc. iii—*continued*

line	*line*
251 BREATHE, exercise	287 TO, compared with
279 JADES, worn-out horses	DARK HOUSE, house for madmen

SCENE V

5 DIAL, watch	67 RESPECTS, motives
54 CLOG, shackle	80 OWE, own
65 PRESENTLY, immediately	

Act Third

SCENE II

31 MISPRISING, despising	118 RAVIN, ravenous
49 QUIRKS, turns	127 OFFIC'D, were the servants
66 ENGROSSEST ALL THE GRIEFS ARE THINE, 'make a corner' in all the griefs as being yours	

SCENE V

S.D. TUCKET, flourish of trumpets	72 BROKES, bargains
20 GO UNDER, pretend to be (*cf. 'went under the name of'*)	91 RING-CARRIER, go-between
36 PALMERS, pilgrims	93 HOST, lodge
69 SHREWD, malicious	99 OF, *after 'worthy the note'*

SCENE VI

3 HILDING, worthless fellow	60 MYSTERY, skill
23 LEAGUER, camp	62 MAGNANIMOUS, great-hearted
35 JOHN DRUM'S ENTERTAINMENT, rough reception (*origin unknown*)	93 EMBOSS'D, exhausted
36 INCLINING, partiality	97 SMOK'D, detected
39 IN ANY HAND, by any means	108 HAVE I' THE WIND, are on the scent of

SCENE VII

line
19 IN FINE, in short
22 COUNTY, count

line
23 SUCCEEDED, descended

Act Fourth

SCENE I

11 LINSEY-WOOLSEY, rough woollen material
19 CHOUGHS, jackdaws
26 PLAUSIVE, plausible
27 SMOKE, suspect

41 BUTTER-WOMAN, type of chatterer and scold
48 AFFORD YOU SO, grant you that
89 WOODCOCK, traditionally foolish bird

SCENE II

3 ADDITION, *with pun on sense of* 'title'

76 COZEN, cheat

SCENE III

16 MONUMENTAL, signet
17 MADE, 'a made man'
COMPOSITION, bargain
28 DIETED, tied down by his appointment
30 COMPANY, companions
ANATOMIZ'D, exposed
31 CURIOUSLY, cunningly
39 HIGHER, further
47 SANCTIMONY, sanctity
83 CONGIED, bidden farewell to
86 MAIN PARCELS OF DISPATCH, dispatching these main affairs
87 NICER, more intimate
95 MODULE, pattern

103 SHED HER MILK, broken the milk jug
122 OUT OF A NOTE, from a questionnaire
137 CHAPE, scabbard
153 LEAVE, die
155 SO MANY, the same
165 CONDITION, standing
176 BOTCHER, patcher (*i.e.* tailor who does repairs)
192 GOOD SADNESS, sober earnest
217 MELL, have intercourse
265 CARDECUE, French silver coin (¼ crown)
FEE-SIMPLE, freehold
276 COMING ON, advancing

GLOSSARY

SCENE IV

line
11 BREAKING, dispersing
23 SAUCY, wanton

line
23 COZEN'D, cheated
35 FINE, end (*finis coronat opus*)

SCENE V

35 FISNAMY, face (physiognomy),
  with perhaps pun on 'name'
41 SUGGEST, lure

51 GATE, road
58 SHREWD, keen
62 PACE, horse's trained gait

Act Fifth

SCENE I

1 POSTING, travelling in haste

32 PRESUME, am sure (*almost* assure you)

SCENE II

8 ALLOW THE
  WIND, don't stand between me
  and the wind

33 CARDECU, quart d'écu, $\frac{1}{4}$ crown,
  about 1/6

SCENE III

4 HOME, truly
10 HIGH fully (*met. from strung bow*)
18 DEAR, precious
29 HATH REFERENCE TO, is to be
  commanded by
72 CESSE, cease
74 DIGESTED, joined
86 REAVE, rob
100 HEAVY, woeful

137 BRIEF, summary
177 FOND, crazy
205 TAX'D, charged
  DEBOSH'D, stained
210 BOARDED, made advances to
231 YOU BOGGLE SHREWDLY, 'you're
  devilish shifty'
292 OWES, owns
294 ABUS'D, deceived
300 EXORCIST, magician